THE KOJO HAND

JD Reed, former Senior Editor, *Time Magazine*, and author of *Free Fall* and *Pursuit of D. B. Cooper*, says of the manuscript: "*The Kojo Hand* is a wonderful novel. It's a kind of *Shane* for baby boomers with a neat twist. Making teacher and student different sexes is a fine touch. Kojo is a truly magnificent character. I wish I'd known him. The cast is great."

John Stewart, Professor of African-American and African Studies, Department of Anthropology, California State University, Davis, and author of *Last Cool Days, Curving Road, For the Ancestors,* and *Looking for Josephine*, says of the manuscript: "The range of experiences and the ways the characters persist in their world are handled with considerable insight. There are some nice things there."

Dr. Marcellette G. Williams, Interim Chancellor and Professor of English and Comparative Literature, The University of Massachusetts, Amherst, says of the manuscript: "Gatten's handling of his female narrator's point of view is deft and refreshingly 'faithful to the grain' (to borrow from Kojo Dedu's phrasing), as is his handling of the narrator's feelings about love in her relationship with her lover, managing even to 'incorporate the knots into the overall design.'"

A NOVEL BY TOM GATTEN

THE KOJO HAND

TOM GATTEN

to Paul J. Dolan
and June Fyfe Gatten

Library of Congress Control Number: 2001126262
ISBN: 0-75961-615-9

This book is printed on acid free paper.

First published in 2001 by 1stBooks Publications, U.S.A.

1st Books Library
2595 Vernal Pike
Bloomington, IN 47404
1stBooks - rev. 9/14/01

"One generation playing its part and passing on,
  Another generation playing its part and passing on in its
    turn…"

WALT WHITMAN,
"Starting from Paumanok,"
Leaves of Grass

"The avid hornet has to dive
  before it enters the transparent lair
  of leaning flowers; to be their
  dream, we must come rising from below."

RAINER MARIA RILKE,
"Graves,"
The Astonishment of Origins

Editor's Note:

The manuscript for this novel and all attendant rights were purchased by the publisher from the estate of Samuel Lyman Crandall, former Professor Emeritus and holder of the Cynthia and Michael Sanders Chair in Comparative Studies in the Department of Anthropology at the State University of New York at Peeze.

The following note was penciled on the title page of the manuscript. Vivian (Vivian Wentworth) was the departmental secretary at the time; Marge (Marge Crandall) was Professor Crandall's wife; Jack (John L. Bergstrom) and Nancy (Nancy P. Newmont) were members of the faculty of the Department of Anthropology.

—Sharon R. Berk
Managing Editor

Vivian—

This manuscript was left on my desk by a student (the author??) during the department Christmas party. As the note says, she wants me "to do something with it" in case she doesn't return after winter break. Please file it in your office with my sabbatical notes, and I'll get back to you about it.

Pleeeeze deposit any checks that come in for me while I'm gone.

Marge and I will have a party next spring when we get back and tell you all about our travels in Ghana—if the headhunters don't get us! Ha!

Have a Happy New Year!

Best,
Sam 12/28/72

P.S. Let Jack know that I returned his precious typewriter to his office, and when Nancy comes in tell her that her books are on the bottom shelf over my desk. Unfortunately, I left the tape recorder I signed out at Allen's Steakhouse. I called the afternoon bartender, Richie, and he said he'd keep it for you. Or maybe you could send a work-study student to get it?

ONE

Deanie watched the receptionist coming in past the young women waiting around the modeling set. She stopped by Deanie, took her glasses off, dropping them to hang from their jeweled safety cord, and waved her notebook overhead to get everyone's attention.

"If you're here for a tryout," the receptionist said, "just put your clothes on a folding chair, and as soon as you put on your tops and earrings sit at a dressing table and Cindy or one of the other models and I will help you with the makeup." She looked at the notebook for a moment. "Who are you?" she said, turning to Deanie.

"I'm Deanie Hollins."

"Let's see," she said, reading her list, "this group is Maria, Teresa, Deanie, Carol–that means you go third, after Teresa."

*   *   *

Now they were at the dressing tables, working with the makeup.

"Try to change your positions every five or ten seconds," Cindy said, looking around at all of them while she brushed Maria's hair. "If you're taking too long or going too fast, the woman with the clipboard will let you know."

"Does Randall expect everybody to pose the way you did all the time or just for the tryout?" Deanie asked.

"Well," she paused, "maybe just the tryout, but let's face it, he has to see a certain look in the photographs. And he didn't tell anybody they *had* to do everything exactly the way I did." She stood there, arranging Maria's hair, lifting and dropping it across her shoulders. "Ya know?"

"How long have you been working here?" Teresa asked.

"Two years," Cindy said.

Carol leaned over to Deanie. "There's your answer," she said. "She's comin' for the boss and, wouldn't you know it, she's still here."

Deanie shrugged and turned back to her mirror. She just didn't have anything to say to Carol right now. She knew that Randall's expectations were a little strange, but maybe there was something to them. Though, she told herself, it was strange that everybody in the whole place seemed so nonchalant about the way they were modeling. But then, if that's the way they always modeled, maybe that's why nobody seemed to pay any attention to them. Even the three girls she came with seemed to accept it as just the way they did things here. She watched Cindy brushing Maria's hair. "Cindy?"

"What?"

"Do *you* model that way all the time, or just when you're showing new girls what Randall expects them to do?" Deanie said.

Cindy raised her eyebrows and stepped back from Maria, and looking towards the mirror reached out to adjust the way

2

Maria's hair fell. "I don't model that way all the time," she said, quietly, without looking at her.

Well, that was something, Deanie thought. From the dressing room doorway Deanie could see the section of the floor in front of Randall's window where the models posed. She stood in the doorway with her arms folded in front of her, wearing a white loosely knitted shawl and a wide-brimmed straw hat, hearing a Rolling Stones tape in the background. She watched Maria modeling a red boatnecked sweater, and she watched the people on the old school chairs sitting around the circle of bright light. Some of them were looking through newspapers, and some of them were just talking and watching. She couldn't tell whether Maria was masturbating or not–it was, she thought, a little strange.

As Teresa went out Deanie moved up to the doorway and watched. She couldn't see Randall because his office window had a dark mirror finish that made it one-way glass. Next to it was another one-way window and she wondered whether anybody was sitting behind it. The two windows looked like a giant pair of mirrored sunglasses resting on the stage. She saw Teresa was having a hard time. She was modeling a pink silk blouse and pink ceramic earrings, and almost every time she changed her position she reached down with her free hand as if to pull a skirt down to cover her legs, and not finding one she would look down as if to see where it had gone and then look surprised. She wished she could do something to help her and she realized how much she herself was shaking from fear of what Randall seemed to expect of her and from fear of losing out on the job that she needed to get to Italy. Now Teresa had both hands stuck down in front of her and the way she squirmed made Deanie wonder what she was trying to do and then she held up an earring that had fallen off and several people applauded and she held the earring higher and stood up and they applauded louder.

"*Olé!*" Teresa shouted. She gestured for the onlookers to join her. "*Olé!*" she shouted. "*Olé!*"

Teresa shook the earring and holding it high paraded around the perimeter of the stage like a bullfighter.

"*Olé!*" two women said in unison as Teresa passed by their table, and several people clapped their hands in approval.

The way Teresa was smiling as she came back to the dressing room lightened the air for Deanie, and she nodded to her as she came in.

"Good recovery," Deanie said.

Teresa dangled the earring in Deanie's face. "*La oreja del toro*," she said. "I kill death."

The statement startled Deanie. "Holy shit," she said. "How do you do that?"

Her face hardened and her eyes narrowed. "You must be very strong." She paused and her face softened. "And you must be able to fake it."

She's something else, she thought, as she watched Teresa walk back to her dressing table and snatch her pantyhose off the chair.

Carol sat smoking a cigarette, examining her nails. The tape had stopped, Cindy and the receptionist had left the dressing room, and Maria was dressed and leaving.

"See you in Randall's office," Maria said. "And good luck."

"Thanks," Deanie whispered. While she sat in the chair on the stage waiting for another tape to play she looked towards the second window wondering whether anyone was on the other side. Now she was looking past the school chairs, trying to avoid looking into anyone's face, and remembering what her high school speech teacher had told her before her first formal five-minute speech. "You don't have to look anyone in the eye if it's going to bother you," he had said. The tape came on. It was Janis Joplin singing "Piece of My Heart" and Deanie took a breath and slid her hand way down the way Cindy had and looked over the school chairs and above the heads on her left to an imaginary line that ran along the paneled wall and across the top part of Randall's window and the other window and across the dressing room door on the other side and around the plastered wall on her right and all the way to Naples, Italy.

"Change," the woman with the clipboard said.

Deanie turned back to her left. *"Just keep scanning across the tops of their heads,"* her teacher was saying, *"and it will look like you've got good eye-contact. You'll look interested in your audience and nobody will know the difference."* She had spent quite a bit of the weekend on the speech and she wanted to do well. Nobody really gave her a hard time because of her age, but being the only sixteen-year-old senior for the early part of the fall did at times make it seem that she was being judged by additional standards, and this was one of those times. Deanie was glad that she had been able to skip a grade, but now standing in front of the speech class she wished she were a junior and with the eleventh grade science classes today on their field trip to the Hayden Planetarium. She scanned the wall over the heads. "If you are planning a trip to Italy," she was saying, "there are four major things to consider—"

"Change," her teacher said.

Deanie looked to her right. *"Customs, climate, companionship, and cash."* She went on with her speech, quoting from a news magazine, her Contemporary Events class notes, and a *Teaneck News-Reporter* column called "Tips for Travelers."

When she was done she sat and listened to four other speeches, and then went home and smoked a joint with her mother.

"Change," the woman with the clipboard said.

Deanie turned to her left and was startled to see the woman photographer right next to her and behind her she saw Bill the limo driver sitting there, smoking a cigarette. People began moving away, putting camera equipment away, turning off lights, and she looked towards the two silvery windows and again was seeing her reflections in the silvery sunglasses and she was on the beach looking up at her history teacher's mirrored sunglasses, gently rocking her thighs against his narrow hips, and then she was remembering that last night over three years ago when she began to realize that he had somebody else, that whatever they had going was almost over.

She could still see the spiral notebook and the pen bent from her grip, digging into the paper. *Why haven't you called me? I can hardly stand it. It's almost midnight and I'm supposed to take your new tennis partner's social studies test tomorrow. I haven't even looked at my notes. But why should I, they're just a lot of circles and loops and YOUR NAME in big block letters. Maybe you'll keep her out past her bedtime and she'll have to call in sick and we won't have the fucking test. Who cares? I don't. Does that surprise you? What the fuck does surprise you? I have this sickening feeling like I've had the dry heaves all day. You know what I'm talking about. It's always like this when things really go wrong with us. I should know better by now. It's like an echo someplace saying, "Deanie, you should have expected this." I don't know, I feel like anything right now would push me past what I could take. Sometimes I want to quit this thing we have together because it's so fucking hard. Too many surprises I can't take. I can't explain it. It's like feelings I can't even describe to myself pushing me towards I don't know what. I don't know where you are or what you're doing, but I don't care. I don't feel anything. I'm pushed in so many directions that I can't feel anything. If I could just have it all go away and wake up not being pushed and pulled in every direction. I go through all these changes to keep from falling over. Falling over what? Falling over myself. If you only knew how much I have to have you. You think I want you to come and save me? From what? From you! So how could you do that? You can't. Though it's sort of happening now, my not feeling, not caring. I wish sometimes until it hurts that we were just friends. You could ask me to tell you about it and I could say it's not important and you could say if you ever want to tell me about it just let me know and you can stop by my office after school. But the way we are it's too much, too much pulling in too many directions. But it still feels like you are there someplace waiting to put up with all this shit. But it's probably because I want you to.*

*   *   *

"Great job," Randall said. "All of you were great." He handed Deanie and Carol each a sandwich as they went into his office. Maria and Teresa were sitting where they had been earlier when they'd all watched Cindy model while Randall went on about what a good job she was doing. Maria was just unwrapping her sandwich. Deanie sat by the door again and Carol walked around to the farthest chair. "Here." He handed a sheet of paper to Maria. "I need your names, addresses, and phone numbers on this before you go."

"Where are the other girls who modeled before we did?" Deanie asked.

"They're working with the receptionist," Randall said, "she's handling their tryouts. Everybody have a soda?" He handed Maria a bottle of soda with a straw in it to pass to Carol and slid one across the desk to Deanie.

They started eating and Maria gave Teresa half of her sandwich, and as Teresa started picking out the lettuce, thick with mayonnaise, and dropping it into a large butt-filled cut-glass ashtray on Randall's desk, he turned his chair towards Deanie and took a bite of his sandwich. An oily blob of mustard dripped past his chin to fall to the seat in the "V" formed by his legs.

Deanie took a bite of her Swiss-on-rye and noticed something moving on her left. Bill, the limo driver who had picked her up that morning, was at the door.

"Ready to go?" he asked.

"Just about," Randall said. He stood up and turned to the wall. "Well—" he said. He reached out and straightened a couple of pictures. "That should do it for today." He walked to the door. "We'll get back to you in two or three days." He

7

turned, holding up the list of names as if it were a guarantee. "Thanks for coming."

"Thanks for coming," Deanie whispered to herself, "canks for thumbing, thanks for coming, banks for slumming, tanks for numbing—boom."

As they got up from their chairs Deanie stared at the triangle of stains on the seat of Randall's chair. He had seen her triangular patch and here was his—mustard, a strand of hair, probably ketchup, tobacco, maybe some grass, some dandruff, spit, coffee, makeup from somebody's face—a regular geologic time chart for anyone who could read the layers. It gave her a funny feeling. It was fascinating in a way, and yet the thought of looking into the layers of Randall's life made her uneasy.

* * *

The ride along the Long Island Expressway had been slow before the Lakeville Road exit, but now they seemed to be making good time. Randall had decided to come along. "I ought to say hello to Barett and Susan," he had said, "and the kid. It's the middle of June already and I haven't seen Susan and Gary since Christmas. And I want to try to meet that African fellow who's teaching out there at Peeze—Kojo something." Kojo something, she had thought, that sounds really strange coming from Randall. His wanting to meet somebody she knew and respected had really surprised her.

Deanie was sitting behind the driver, looking out the window and trying to imagine what on earth Randall and Kojo could possibly have to talk about. Randall sat on her right, a bag of ice between his feet, sipping a Scotch-and-soda that he had made from a small supply of liquor and mix that he kept in a bar cabinet built into the back of the front seat. Deanie had a lime soda with a little vodka in it.

"That African fellow. What's his name? Kojo—" He opened and closed his hand over his closed thumb as if he were trying to milk an answer from the air.

"Kojo Dedu?" she said.

"Dedu," he said. "That's right."

"He teaches in the Comparative Culture Program."

"That's right. Oral literature, film."

"Poetry," she said.

"Do you know him?"

"A little. Sometimes when a class was really involved with something, he'd invite everyone to his apartment to continue the discussion."

"So you had a class from him. When was that?"

"Last fall."

"How was it?"

"It was really interesting, but I had to drop it."

"How come?"

"My mother got really sick and I've had to go home a lot. Which is why I'm in summer school—I had to drop a course, and now I need the credits in order to have junior standing for the study-abroad program this fall."

Randall sat looking into his drink. "Must've been rough."

Deanie nodded. She rested her head back and looked out towards the jagged line cut by trees and tops of buildings along the sky. She longed to be up there heading into the blue...passing through. She wondered why Randall would want to see Kojo. There was still something about Randall's speaking of Kojo that made her feel uncomfortable. It was, for one thing, something about his voice. She couldn't say exactly what. She watched a station wagon full of kids in the next lane dropping behind them, and she saw one of the kids pushing his face flat against the window. It was something like that, she thought. It was as if Randall's words themselves flattened Kojo's image, made it two dimensional. Maybe it was everything that had happened today that made her uncomfortable. She looked back out at the jagged line of treetops and buildings. Zig-zagging up and down, up and down—and watching the jagged line she remembered walking up the steps in the Port Authority bus terminal this morning. She had walked out and stood on the

9

curb, looking into the noisy Eighth Avenue traffic. And now she was there again, watching for the limousine. She slid her frayed sneaker towards the suitcase, opened the red umbrella against the sunny June sky, and hooked her thumb over the top of her faded jeans. She was posing. Not much, she thought, just enough to start getting psyched up for the modeling job that would, if it worked out, give her the money she needed by the end of the summer for her junior year in Italy. She adjusted the shoulder strap of the small leather bag at her hip and moved the umbrella to her other shoulder. She could still see her mother in the driveway in Teaneck this morning, fidgety in her cotton housecoat, worried that the job might not work out, that the school in Naples might be too difficult.

"It just seems like you're trying to do too much," her mother had said.

"Don't worry," she had said, "it's not really an academic thing—the university's 'Junior Year in Italy' program is just a convenience. Going to Naples is something I have to do. You know that. I've been talking about it since I was a junior in high school."

"I know," her mother had said, "ever since you slept with your history teacher."

"That's history."

"*Oy vay*," she moaned, throwing her hands in the air.

"I mean that was all over and done with a long time ago."

Her mother sighed. "But what if this modeling job doesn't work out?"

"I could waitress again," she had said. "But then I'd probably have to rob a bank or something. But don't worry. I told you I'll be working for Barett's brother. And I'll be home a time or two before summer session is over. What could possibly keep me from going to Italy?"

"There's always something," her mother had said, self-consciously folding her arms across her chest as if to hide the fact of her recent mastectomy.

She impatiently tapped her foot, twirled the umbrella that was supposed to identify her and remembered, as she often did, how Barett Burkhart, one of her profs at the state university at Peeze out on Long Island, had told her about the job.

"It's a sure thing," he was saying. "I've talked to Randall and it's all set."

"What does that mean?" she said.

"You've got a tryout, and, if he's got any sense at all, he'll hire you." He went on to describe his brother's modeling and advertising agency that was somewhere on West 54th Street. "Good hours, damn good pay, and you'll be able to go to summer school," Barett said. "You'll have all the opportunities of the Big Apple and all the advantages of Long Island's beautiful north shore." His voice was full of promise, and she couldn't help smiling at the prospects. Then he wheezed a little laugh roughened by cigarette smoke, and clinking the ice cubes in his tall vodka and tonic had said, "You're in like Flynn."

She could see a black limo cutting into the line of taxis and she impatiently switched the umbrella to her other shoulder, flipped her long blond hair back from her dangling earrings, straightened her gray Mickey Mouse T-shirt, and watched the limo with heavily tinted windows stop in front of her. The window went down and gradually she saw the driver's long hair, pale complexion, part of a smile—he said something to the man next to him and glanced back and forth a couple of times. "Cheekbones are right up there. Gray-blue eyes. Long legs," he said.

The man next to him said something.

"Are you the lady with the red umbrella?" the driver asked.

"Do you see anybody else with one?"

"I guess not."

"Do you work for Randall Burkhart?"

"He's sitting right here."

"Are you Deanie Hollins?" the faceless man asked.

"Yes," she said, taking down the umbrella.

The driver got out and without any introductions walked to the rear of the limousine and waited for her to bring her suitcase back. She gave him the umbrella, and as he hoisted the suitcase into the trunk he pointed at the green and white decal of the treble clef design with the words "Stan Kenton" across it in script.

"You a Kenton fan?" he asked.

"This was my father's suitcase."

"He played with Kenton?"

"For a while," she said. "He sat in for somebody who got pneumonia or something."

"What was his axe?"

"What did he ask?"

"What did he play?"

"'Artistry in Rhythm,' 'A Little Jive is Good for You'—" He frowned and seemed to be studying the trunk lid's locking mechanism. "Trombone," she said.

"That must have been a gas," he said. "I'm not exactly a big band nut, but that must have been somethin' else, blowin' with those cats."

"You must be a musician."

The limousine horn honked twice and he slammed the trunk lid.

"I play a little piano," he said.

"So do I," she said, and he turned away without responding.

He was in the driver's seat before Deanie reached the open rear door. It seemed strange that the driver looked the way he did, yet sounded like her dad who got flat-top haircuts and still said "crazy" when he meant "all right" and "threads" when he meant "clothes."

As they pulled into traffic Deanie settled on the drop seat hinged to the rear of the front seat and smiled at the three girls facing her. She hadn't expected anyone else. She heard music playing and saw that Randall Burkhart had slid back the divider window. He had a tape cartridge in his hand and pointing it like a flashlight at each of them introduced himself and the three others. The two with black hair and Spanish accents were Maria and Teresa, and the bleached blond was Carol. Deanie rested her hands on her knees and leaned out to make eye contact with him, smiled, and turned to the three others. "I'm Deanie," she said.

Randall did look like Barett—though Barett had a full beard, and Randall had only a neatly trimmed moustache. She knew he was a couple of years older than Barett, but he didn't look it. His dark blond hair was styled to cover the top third of his ears. Barett's hair was more curly than straight and usually looked like it had been cut with dull hedge clippers. Deanie pushed her hair back from her ears and turned to the others. Maria wore a bright yellow dress and yellow sandals. Teresa had a white blouse with lots of frills, a short skirt, light blue, and spike heels, blue with silver flecks. Carol was wearing a white cotton turtleneck, a pink skirt, and penny loafers.

"Do you work for"—Deanie hesitated—"Mr. Burkhart?"

"'Randall' is okay," he interrupted.

"Maybe," Maria said. "Who knows?"

"They're going for a tryout too," he said to her. "Only their connection is a little less formal than yours." He looked back at the others. "She's a friend of my brother." His voice was in the tenor range, a little higher than Barett's.

"My cousin works in his building," Maria said, pointing at Randall. "One night we came to see him and Mr. Burkhart discovered us."

Teresa nodded vigorously.

"I was standing on the sidewalk in front of Bloomingdale's," Carol said. "I had just come from their personnel office when Randall and the driver came up to me and told me about the agency. And they showed me my picture in some opportunity layouts."

Before Deanie could ask what opportunity layouts were, Carol showed them to her. They were eight-by-ten photographs mounted on plastic sheets, photographs of models in indoor and outdoor scenes. Some of the original faces had been cut out and behind the cut-out faces somebody, Randall, she assumed, had taped Polaroid snapshots of the three others. The layouts reminded her of the painted scenes of cowboys and bathing beauties they have at fairs and carnivals for people to stick their heads through to be photographed.

"There I am," Maria said, "there I am." She pointed excitedly to a fur-coated model bearing her face and standing by a Rolls-Royce. "And I didn't even know he took my picture until he showed me."

Maria shuffled through the layouts so Deanie could see them—Teresa in a polo outfit standing by a handsome man on a horse, Carol in a string bikini leaning voluptuously against the mast of a sailboat—all kinds of romantic pictures. For a moment Deanie pictured herself arriving in Italy. She recalled, as if hearing a persistent echo, the voice of the man who had been her ninth-grade history teacher telling her about the beauty and romance of the country. He went there every summer and every time he came back he had wonderful stories to tell her about all the things she could see and do there. Back in high school anything seemed better than Teaneck, New Jersey, and his stories made Naples seem out of this world. And now, as much as she tried to cope with living in uncertainty, there were still times when anywhere seemed better than wherever she was at the moment, though Naples was always the special place in her imagination, and with the thought of it she took a deep breath of anticipation.

There seemed to be less traffic now. She heard the end of "American Pie" and the tape stopped playing. Nobody was talking. Suddenly Randall yelled for the driver to stop. Deanie turned to see Randall holding a camera by his face as he pushed his door open. She didn't know exactly where in lower Manhattan they were. She saw an old woman in a winter coat sitting on a blanket on the sidewalk. A little past her two puffy-faced men stood drinking from bottles in brown bags. She watched Randall take a couple of pictures of another old man walking towards them.

"He wants to get some pictures of his face," the driver said. "I'll open the window so we can hear better." Teresa's window slid down and Deanie turned with the others to watch the old man coming closer.

Almost every store window he passed was held together by strips of brown tape. Behind him a swirl of papers eddied up from the gutter and rushed into a doorway and rolled out to fall flopping on the sooty sidewalk. The old man stopped and watched Randall approaching him. Randall stopped next to him, and the old man tapped the front of his brown stocking cap in a little salute and continued on his way.

"Wait a minute. I'd like to get a picture," Randall said.

The old man straightened his oversized tweed jacket, tucked the front of his shirt into his baggy pants, and kept walking.

"Just a second, please."

The old man stopped, looking straight ahead.

Randall glanced back over his shoulder and the driver pulled the limo up next to them.

"I'm taking some photographs for some charity projects."

The old man turned around. "Whose?"

"Lots of them," Randall said. "It won't take a minute."

The old man looked down and seemed to be thinking. Randall squatted and took another picture. The old man started walking.

"Hey, buddy, what's it worth to ya?" Randall said.

The old man stopped. Already six people were standing back against the store front to watch. He looked towards Randall. "What kind of charity did you say?"

"All kinds. Overnight shelters, soup kitchens, Salvation Army. We're putting together some pictures that they're going to use to raise money for 'em. We're taking pictures all over the city."

"Five bucks," the old man said.

"Okay. Now can you move around a little?"

"Where's the money?"

"When we're done," Randall said. "As God and those people in the limo are my witnesses."

The old man stood looking towards the limousine. Deanie wondered if he could see her sitting there.

"Now move around a little," Randall said.

"How do you mean?"

"Can you stumble around in a circle like you were drunk?"

"I can try."

He started turning around.

"No. Wait a minute," Randall said. "Don't pivot. Walk around in a circle. Imagine one knee is stiff and you have a nail punched through your other shoe."

The old man started taking long, wobbly steps in a circle. Randall moved around squatting, shooting, crouching, and shooting.

"A little faster," Randall said.

The old man sped up and held his arms out for balance.

"Great. Keep it up," Randall said, still shooting. Along the store fronts there were a dozen people watching. "Now take your cap off."

The old man pulled his cap off and held it way up, taking wider and faster steps. His heavy white hair swung back and forth across his ruddy cheeks.

"Great," Randall said. He backed away and got into the limo. The door slammed, and the old man caught himself on a lamppost and stopped his swinging foot against a wire trash basket.

"You really had me—" He was breathing hard. "You really had me going there."

"You'd make a great dancer," Randall said.

"Five bucks, wasn't it?"

Randall threw something out the window and took another picture. Deanie leaned closer to the window and saw the old man picking up a coin. Randall took three pictures in quick succession.

"You're four dollars and seventy-five cents short."

"Sorry, twinkle-toes, that's it. Take it or leave it." He took another picture.

"You bastard," he said, lunging against the limo and shooting his arm in to hit Randall in the face. The horn honked and the door kicked open throwing the old man off balance and Randall jumped out and smashed him across the ear with a windshield brush. He belched gurgling pain and tottered back dumping the trash basket. He came back fast, grabbing the basket and swinging it at Randall who ducked behind the door to block the hit. Randall spun around the door to swing his leg across the backs of the old man's knees, dropping him in the trash.

Randall jumped back in the seat and the tires screeched. Deanie felt her stomach tightening as the limo roared ahead. That poor man, she thought, wondering if anybody was helping him. A few doors up the block the driver let up on the gas and Randall twisted around to open the partially closed door and slam it shut.

Deanie watched her companions glancing at each other, and Randall turned around holding a handkerchief to his nose.

"He didn't have to hit me," he said. "I wanted to get his facial expressions when he thought he was only getting a quarter. I was going to give him the five bucks." He held up a handful of dollar bills. "Ten bucks as a matter of fact. He didn't have to hit me." He looked directly at each of them, and turned to the driver. "Right, Bill?"

"Right," the driver said, "he even had the money on the seat before he got out."

Randall turned back to them. He looked as if he was going to say "See, I told you so," but he only shrugged, glanced at the driver, and looked back again. "No sense of humor," he said.

"Maybe. Who knows?" Teresa said.

"My nose," Randall said, pointing at his bloody handkerchief. "My nose knows, goddamnit."

He turned back to the front and punched in another tape.

Deanie slouched forward and sliding her hands across her knees looked at the others sitting with her wondering what they were thinking. But as the Rolling Stones' "Sympathy for the Devil" came on nobody said anything.

*   *   *

As they got out of the limousine in front of an office of the Chase Manhattan Bank, Deanie took a couple of deep breaths to compose herself. Randall Burkhart rolled up the sleeves of his white shirt, and as he hitched up his light gray pants he told the driver to keep Deanie's suitcase, get gassed up, and come back at three-thirty to take Maria and Teresa home and then drive Deanie out to her place on Long Island.

"That's the limo I want gassed up," he said, "not you."

The driver saluted and closed the window.

Randall Burkhart led Deanie and the two others past the bank and into the pink granite lobby of the office building, past the doorman, to the elevators. Randall stood back and gestured for them to go in. Deanie saw that he was in fact shorter than Barett, maybe five-nine. His shoulders were slightly rounded, lowering his dark brown eyes to the level of hers as he smiled and turned in behind her.

The elevator door opened on the fourth floor. Teresa took a step and screamed. A silver streak flashed past Deanie's face, through the doorway, and Randall was slashing "Z's" in the air with a switchblade.

"What?" he shouted. "What?"

Deanie backed next to Maria and Carol and saw that Teresa's spike heel had caught in the space between the elevator floor and the building floor.

"My heel's stuck," Teresa said.

"But why did you scream?" Randall asked.

"It scared me."

"Who knows?" Maria said.

Randall looked at Maria, rolled his eyes in a look of disbelief, pocketed the knife, and dropped to one knee to work on the heel. As he worked her foot back and forth, Teresa held her skirt down with one hand, steadied herself on the edge of the elevator, and wiggled her hips with each twist of her foot for the benefit, Deanie thought, of the blue-uniformed security guard who was coming around the corner to his desk right in front of the elevator.

Randall freed the heel and leaned back with a sigh.

"Thank you," Teresa said.

"Think nothing of it," Randall said.

Deanie watched to see how Randall got up, if he would brush Teresa's thigh, or if he would look her in the eyes as he stood up, but it was a clean break. Though, Deanie reflected, she could have stepped out of her shoe to begin with. So maybe her wiggling was for Randall.

"Where were you when I needed you?" Randall said, pointing at the guard.

"I heard the scream," he said, "but then I saw you from the doorway." He pointed. "And I saw you had everything"—he paused and snapped his fingers on both hands—"workin' out." He smiled and winked at Teresa. She lifted her head as if she was reading something on the ceiling as the four of them followed Randall Burkhart toward the reception area of Burkhart Modeltronics, Inc.

The reception area bloomed with soft lights and a variety of large-leafed tropical-looking plants that seemed to grow from everywhere. The receptionist looked up from her desk and leaned towards them, the strong yellow cast of her hair and her pushed-up nose making her look a little like a tiger. The whole room resembled the print of a Rosseau painting Deanie had seen in the library at Peeze.

Randall said something to the receptionist and she nodded.

Deanie had never been behind the scenes in the world of modeling and advertising. Though as they moved towards the door marked "Studio A" she remembered posing in the fifth grade along with several other children by a huge pile of pumpkins. They were being photographed to publicize some sort of autumn fund raiser for the hospital, something sponsored by the Friends of Mercy. She had just begun to wonder whether she had ever been paid for posing and, if she had, whether her mother had kept the money or put it in her piggy bank, or what, when the studio door opened and loud music rushed at them from way on the other side where a line of fully costumed cancan dancers kicked their feet high under bright lights. Randall motioned for them to follow. The door shut behind them, and the studio was dark except for the stage lights way across. The studio smelled of glue and paint and cigarette smoke. As Deanie's eyes adjusted she saw a few spectators by the dancers and closer a scattering of folding chairs and closer sections of stage sets and closer still costumes piled on a table and Teresa screamed.

"What?" Randall shouted.

Deanie turned to see Teresa standing by a shadowy airplane that was about six feet off the floor, suspended from somewhere in the darkness overhead.

"I thought that goddamn thing was going to land on my head," Teresa said.

Randall sighed and brushed back his hair.

"It's okay now," Deanie said.

"That's what I say," Randall said. He winked at her. "Now let's all go to my office." He pointed in the direction of the dancers. Why did he wink at me? she asked herself, seeing Randall wait for her as the others headed for the office.

"Have you ever seen a biplane?"

"I've seen pictures," she said.

"This is a two-thirds scale model of a Stearman Trainer," he said proudly. He reached up and spun a wheel. "That was the main biplane of the 30's and 40's. My crew built this in two weeks. We used it for a network shampoo ad and for a local bank ad in Phoenix. Now we're going to cut it in half for a cold medicine ad. The plane will separate in the middle and the pilot will reach back and catch hold of the sneezing passenger—'Get it together with Mentho Mist!'" Wide-eyed with enthusiasm he reached out and pretended to grope for her hand, as if to pull her into his imaginary flight. Instinctively, she leaned away, and he turned for his office.

Randall's office faced the studio through a big floor-to-ceiling window with beige drapes covering the whole lower half. Around the maroon carpet dark wood shelves of books and binders ran waist high against the other three walls, and over the top shelves hung framed photographs of people shaking hands with him. Above the photographs were his diploma from The Ohio State University, College of Administrative Science—Master of Business Administration—and a variety of brass-plated advertising-award plaques in the shapes of stars, rectangles, and hearts. From the far wall at the other end of the window, four orange and red stuffed swivel chairs curved out facing the window. After a chair-width space sat his desk, also facing the window. A fifth orange and red swivel chair, its back to the window, was by the end of the desk in front of Deanie. Randall asked her to sit in it and pointed towards the chairs past the other end of the desk for the others.

"Grab a chair," he said, walking out the door.

That was just like Barett, she thought. He'd schedule students for conferences, arrive after they'd gathered by his door, seat two or three in his office, shuffle some papers, and then leave, saying he'd be right back. Then two minutes before he had to leave for his next class he'd return, apologizing for being tied up by the bureaucracy.

Deanie stood by her chair and with the three others watched the last of the cancan dancers leave the stage. Two workmen followed them off, pushing a huge model of a beer bottle that was twice their height. Randall came back, shut the office door, and sat at the desk. Deanie swiveled her chair around and she and the others sat down.

"Is anybody hungry?" he said. He switched on a tape deck on his desk and began looking through a stack of tapes.

21

Nobody answered.

"Nobody wants anything?" he said. He turned from Deanie to the three others and back to her.

"I could eat something," she said.

Maria and Carol nodded agreement, and Randall took the orders for sandwiches and sodas and repeated them to somebody on the intercom.

"Okay," Randall said. "Now here's how it works." He looked from side to side at the four of them. "Right now we're interested in the three 'P's'—purpose, passion and perception." He paused to adjust his watch. "And profit," he added, "but that goes without saying. And at any rate another 'P' would cause confusion with what we call *the* 'Four P's'"—he pointed to the ceiling for emphasis—"price, product, promotion, and path, which you'll learn about if you stay with Modeltronics, especially if you become involved with marketing."

Deanie couldn't tell whether Randall was trying to sound important, or if he was trying to focus their attention on the fact that he ran a business and that they were there for tryouts for jobs.

"So," he said. "Purpose, passion, and perception. We'll take care of purpose. It's up to you to successfully demonstrate the other two, passion and perception. In other words, show us how well you can get into the mood and how you see yourselves as serious models." He looked from side to side again. "First we'll watch Cindy. She's been with us for a while and she'll demonstrate what I'm talking about. Then two other girls are here to try out, just like you are, and they'll do their thing, and then you can go to the dressing room and you can have a chance. And don't worry, all the photographs will be from the waist up." Deanie wondered why Randall had said that. He adjusted his watch again and called somebody on the intercom. "Let's get started." He punched a tape into the deck and asked Deanie to swivel around and hit the light switch on the wall. She swiveled around and stood up and flicked off the lights. Standing there she saw that the twelve or fourteen people who had been watching the cancan dancers were still sitting along the edge of the area where she and the others were going to try out. A couple of people were on folding chairs and all the rest sat on desk chairs. School chairs, she thought. Some of the people were reading newspapers, a couple of the women were leafing through magazines, and a man sitting just on the other side of the office window was drinking a soda. She wondered who they were. A woman wearing a navy blue suit, horn-rimmed glasses, and carrying a clipboard dragged a wide padded chair across the polished wood floor to the center of the photo set, and from overhead a white backdrop unrolled, coming down to meet the floor behind the chair. Deanie turned to see Randall looking at her. "Those people all work here," he said. "They come to all of the tryouts."

Deanie nodded and sat down. Across the drapes she saw a couple of floodlight stands moving into place, a camera that must have been on a tripod, the head and shoulders of a man adjusting the camera, and the wide-brimmed straw hat, face, and loosely knitted red net shawl of a model came into view as she walked onto the stage. She sank down, apparently to sit on the chair, leaving only her hat, head, and shoulders visible above the drapes.

She tilted the hat back and looked to her right to give a profile to the camera and the photographer squeezed a shutter switch on the end of a cord he held cheek-high and she slid her hand behind her neck and around and down across the shawl and she looked towards the camera and the photographer squeezed the switch again and she slid down in the chair and tipped the hat forward. She sat up and tilted the hat back and as she kept changing poses a woman with a camera moved in and out of view taking pictures. Both photographers took quite a few pictures.

"Pay close attention to her facial expressions," Randall said. "Notice how sexy she looks. What she's projecting will jump right off the page. People will want to feel the way *she's* feeling and they'll buy whatever she's wearing to feel that way too."

Randall glanced towards the three others on his left and then to Deanie. "You can open the drapes now."

Deanie leaned forward and felt behind the drapes for the cord and started pulling it hand over hand. The drapes were opening, and she was pulling the cord hand over hand *and now she was pulling a rope hand over hand over a pulley and one of the cows in her uncle's barn had her legs tied to the stall posts and the vet was reaching way up inside her for the calf who seemed to have been tangled up and,* the cord stopped, the drapes open, she felt shock deep within her, and baffled almost to tears took a deep breath and relaxed enough to suppose that there must be some sort of reason the model wasn't wearing anything under the shawl and a reason she was rubbing her crotch while with her other hand she still tilted the hat this way and that.

Carol was biting her knuckles, Maria was leaning forward, resting her chin in her hands, her elbows on her knees, and Teresa sat up straight with her hands in her lap. Randall was tapping the pencil on his forehead. Deanie looked back at the model. She was rolling her head back and forth on the back of the chair. Deanie wondered if she was supposed to be acting out Randall's idea of orgasm, and Randall looked as if he knew what she was thinking.

"That's real," he said. "Cindy is something else. That's what you should all shoot for—the real thing."

She could hardly believe what she was seeing. Randall seemed so sincere, yet his excitement made her wonder. And when she looked away from him at the people sitting around the stage, everybody seemed so indifferent. Is this for real? she asked herself. The next model came out of the shadows at the far side of the stage. She wore a short light-green terry cloth robe and had the most beautiful hair that Deanie had ever seen. It was dark and thick and long with a magnificent natural curl and she knew how to carry it, but when she began touching herself she kept looking up towards the ceiling and the photographers only took a couple of pictures before walking away.

The next model out wore a yellow turtleneck and big red and white ceramic earrings and had her blond hair up in a ponytail. As she sat down she hitched up her short skirt and as she started getting into the posing Deanie held her hands up to frame a head and shoulders picture and tried to imagine how it would look as an earring ad in a magazine. After a few moments the model began taking deep breaths and drawing back the corners of her mouth.

"Atta girl," Randall said, pressing his clenched fist to the desk.

She began rolling her head from side to side and the photographers were busy moving and shooting. Suddenly she jerked her neck and Deanie heard her yelp over the music and through the glass.

"That's it! That's it!" Randall said, pounding his fist on the desk. "That's great!"

* * *

In the dressing room the model who had gone first and the receptionist from the front desk gave Deanie and the three others tops and earrings to model.

"Do you want a drink, another ice cube?" Randall was asking.

"What?"

"Do you want a drink, some more ice?"

"I'm okay," Deanie said, "thanks."

"You looked like you were lost in thought."

Deanie shrugged. "Not really," she said.

Now she was noticing the passing traffic and listening to Randall talk about all kinds of things. At first she wondered whether Randall was really interested in talking to her or if he was working around to hitting on her. She knew people sometimes misunderstood her and often underestimated her intelligence, but as he went on, and as she occasionally responded with a comment or a question, it soon seemed that Randall Burkhart was sincere, that he enjoyed talking to her—which was strange, she thought, because she certainly didn't enjoy talking to him. But maybe he wasn't as weird as he had seemed back at the agency. The really strange thing was that he acted like the tryouts had never even happened.

He wanted to meet Kojo to try to get a look at the media market and the culture market through Kojo's eyes. Barett had told him that Kojo once ran a film company in West Africa, and Randall thought that maybe in talking with Kojo he could discover some tribal instincts that he might translate for his own use at Modeltronics.

"For one thing, I'm trying to get a better handle on holism," Randall said, "you know, one and one is three, two and two is five—I want to market that."

The idea of Randall's borrowing anything from Kojo's experience to put to his own use still bothered her. She couldn't picture Kojo working with Randall on anything, but it was also true that an hour ago she didn't know that Kojo had run a film company. He stopped talking to make another drink, and after flipping the intercom switch a couple of times, tapped on the glass divider. The driver slid the window back a few inches. "You okay, Bill?" Randall asked.

The driver gave a thumbs-up sign and closed the window.

Randall kept talking, and every so often he said something about his personal life that touched on his brother's family, Barett and his wife Susan and their son Gary, Barett's child from a former marriage.

Deanie had known Barett since she started at Peeze. As her advisor he was supposed to sign all of the paperwork required for registration and financial aid. He advised her to take his section of Freshman Composition, so she saw him often, and as time went on she became a frequent guest at the Burkharts' place on the Sanborn estate. Before long Deanie was the primary sitter for Gary when Barett and Susan went out, or when Susan went to her job in Manhattan twice a week.

She had come to know Barett and Susan pretty well, she thought, and now Randall was going on about their family—he and Barett had no other brothers or sisters, Randall had been divorced and had no children, they had grown up in Steubenville, Ohio. After Randall got his M.B.A. from Ohio State he joined the army and went into the Quartermaster Corps. He had wanted to see how he could use military strategy in marketing, and at the same time he wanted to get his military obligation out of the way.

"To make a long story short," he said, "creating a need in the other side—enemy, market, or whatever—is a lot like putting a hole in it. But I didn't learn that in the Quartermaster Corps." He paused, as if reflecting. "I did learn about massive reorganization"—he made a stirring motion with his hand—"we reorganized the whole goddamn Quartermaster Corps into the Material Command before I got out."

Deanie saw the Hicksville exit and knew that it would be about forty-five minutes to Port Jefferson and then another twenty minutes to Peeze Point. When she rested her head back on the seat and shut her eyes Randall stopped talking. Something he had said echoed for a moment at the edge of her consciousness bringing back memories of a party at her neighbor's house on a Labor Day afternoon three or four years ago. Her neighbor and five other guys who had graduated the previous June were having an impromptu farewell party for themselves and six other guys. They were all going away to college or the army and probably Vietnam in the coming week. Deanie and her girlfriends had hung out with them over the years and she wanted to say goodbye and when she went next door she was the only girl there. And as the afternoon went on they started fooling around and when she wanted to stop they wouldn't let her. When it was all over she felt really out of it and, puzzled and angry, she swore she'd never let herself get drawn into something like that again.

She looked at Randall and the driver and warily set her drink on the floor. Now Randall was looking out the window. She looked past him, through the tinted glass that darkened the trees. She saw an orange and silver U-Haul truck by the side of the road, its hood up, the green tops of trees, vapor trails. She pictured herself and a friend sailing through the sky ahead of a vapor trail. Who could it be? She couldn't picture a face, she could just feel someone at her side. She hoped it was her friend Zerk, the two of them going way out and beyond the blue.

TWO

It was almost seven o'clock when they drove between the massive stone gateposts of the old Harris Sanborn estate. From the gateposts the dirt drive into the grounds curved towards the gatehouse and headed towards the mansion in the center of the property. Barett and Susan rented one half of the mansion, now a duplex, built in the early 1800's, and the present-day Sanborns, a couple in their early fifties, lived in the other half when they weren't in Florida or upstate New York. Deanie lived in the gatehouse, a nine-room frame house that the Sanborns were converting into studio apartments—and because the reconstruction went on so sporadically they asked very little rent from her. Barett had told her about the place, and as soon as she saw it she took the upstairs apartment.

As they passed the gatehouse Deanie saw Jacob the gray-haired carpenter in bib overalls sitting on the gate of his green

29

pickup, smoking a pipe, the unpruned apple and peach trees lined up along the drive. Between the gatehouse and the mansion was a long shake-shingled apartment, originally a stable, where her friend Zerk Lewis lived, and spread across the grounds were a barn, two sheds, and a window-walled artist's studio where various Sanborns, not having to work for a living, had tried their hands at painting and sculpture. Looking past Randall's head to the fruit trees reminded her of the many Sanborn paintings–they had looked like American folk art—she had seen at tag sales around St. James and Setauket when she was furnishing her apartment. A dark green Volvo sat nosing the screen door of Zerk's place. He must have company, she thought. His kitchen and living room lights were on. That's good, she could hardly wait to see him.

The driver parked the limo on the crushed-rock section of the drive that ran along the side of the mansion and then looped back to rejoin itself about thirty yards towards the main gate.

"Okay, Bill," Randall said, "come back in an hour or so. We'll probably stay overnight." Deanie got out and followed Randall. He stopped by Barett's station wagon and looked in. "He still carries his golf clubs around with him and he hasn't played in years. Or has he?"

"I don't know," Deanie said. She had seen the clubs there before, but she hadn't thought about why they were there. She knew that Barett had mentioned golf as something that he used to do once in a while—until, according to Susan, his habit of walking around with his custom-made putter led to his getting his hand broken in four places. He had gone into a bar in Queens called the Elbow Inn and apparently the name of the place went to his head. Right in the middle of a pool game Barett jumped up on the pool table and putted in the eight-ball to the dismay of the two hard hats who had stopped by on their way home from work for a leisurely game of pool and a couple pitchers of beer.

Susan hadn't known Barett then—they had first met when he was finishing up his Ph.D. at Columbia—but she knew of the incident and had mentioned it on more than one occasion as they prepared to go out for the evening while Deanie sat with Gary.

A slight breeze bent the tops of the forsythia against the mansion's stones and across the window screens along the path to the kitchen entrance. Deanie brushed her hand along the shrubs and felt the leaves as Randall crunched ahead on the crushed rock to the steps where Susan Burkhart was just appearing from behind the screen door.

She was wearing tan culottes, a long-sleeved white pullover, and her extremely fine brown hair fluttered across her freckled cheeks. She brushed the hair back from her face and smiled at Deanie.

"Who have you got here, Randall?" Her words, as usual, were soft and measured, her voice mellowed from cigarillo smoke. She put her hand out for him and bent over for his kiss on the cheek. As she straightened up in the fading light and pushed open the door, her thin, supple figure seemed almost a part of the swaying forsythia by the steps.

"You're looking well," Randall said.

"And so are you," she said. "I was delighted when Barett said you'd called. And Gary's already drawn you a picture."

"We'll have to see that," he said.

"And, Deanie," Susan said, as Randall went inside, "how was the tryout?"

"It was different."

"Different? How so?" She looked puzzled.

"Well, let's just say it was sort of like a high school speech class."

Susan looked really bewildered. "I don't get it."

"It was just different, that's all, a new experience."

"Well," Susan said, "did you get the job?"

Deanie shrugged. "He said he'd get back to us in two or three days."

"Randall," Susan said, as Deanie went in past her, "did Deanie—"

"Of course she got the job," he said. "She was great. I thought she knew that." He looked at Deanie. "Okay?"

She nodded. "Thanks. Thank you."

Deanie heard one of Barett's Beach Boys albums as she followed Randall through the cluttered kitchen and darkened dining room into the bright living room, recently painted a light green. Barett Burkhart sat in a blue wing-back chair with a stack of newspapers on his lap. As usual he was reading a *Daily News* sports page. He stood up to greet them, threw his hands to his mouth to cover a cough, and the papers cascaded to a pile on the braided rug.

"Whoops," he said. He stepped over the papers and extended his hand to Randall. Barett was at least a head taller than his brother. "How've you been?"

Randall said something, and Gary came in with a picture he'd drawn on a sheet of typing paper. Barett said hello to Deanie, took the needle off the record, coughed, clicked off the amplifier, and sat down. Barett filled the chair, and when he picked Gary up and sat him on his knee the two of them looked like models for a Santa Claus sketch—the full-bearded, big-bellied guy with baggy pants nodding towards the little kid whose drawing might have been a gift list. And behind the kid Randall might have been an interested parent reading the list over his shoulder.

Susan brought Randall a drink and sat by Deanie on an antique love seat stuffed with horsehair that had begun to work its way out of a split seam in the worn velvet. In the weeks that Deanie had been away in Teaneck the Sanborns had hired someone to paint over the living room wallpaper and refinish the pine floors, and Susan explained in detail how the work had gone. When they started talking about faceless university administrators and McGovern's presidential campaigning Deanie found herself, as she often did, taking Gary upstairs to help him get ready for bed.

He was, Deanie thought, a good kid—though a little nervous. But he had been through some heavy changes since his mother's death when he was four. She sat on the edge of the bed and rested her head in her hands while Gary started putting on his pajamas. She was tired.

"Which is the front?" he asked. He stood before her holding out the top of his pajamas.

Deanie held up the pullover top. "It doesn't make any difference," she said, handing it back, "just put it on."

"Are you going to read me a story?"

"Sure."

*   *   *

As Deanie went down the steps she could tell that they were talking family talk "—the house in Steubenville...Grandpa Burkhart's Civil War discharge papers," and she heard Randall going on about college football and wondering aloud whether Susan had ever participated in a cheering section. As she went into the living room Susan was shaking her finger at Randall.

"I have *never* participated in a *cheering* section in my *life*."

There was a slight pause in the conversation, and Barett asked Randall why he wanted to meet Kojo now. He looked at Deanie as if he had changed the subject of the conversation in deference to her.

"After all," Barett said, "he's been at Peeze for three years— not counting the year he went back to Africa on a so-called research project."

"His going back wasn't a so-called anything," Susan said. "He had to go in and out to maintain his visa status."

Barett raised his eyebrows. "He had to go in and out?" He chuckled, Deanie thought, at the double meaning he found in the phrase, and reached for a pack of cigarettes on the end table. He turned back with a self-satisfied smile, put a cigarette to his lips, and lit it, looking across the flame towards Susan. "In and out," he said slowly, extending his jaw to let the smoke roll across his mustache and up his nostrils.

Susan sighed, glanced towards the ceiling, and looked at Randall.

"Well," Randall said, "you know I'm always looking for new ideas, and—when was it?—last October I saw that article in the Sunday paper about his work in African art, and that just clicked as something to look into. And I've been wanting to say hello to you and Susan and Gary, and today I had a ride to your door."

"And good company," Susan said, extending her arm towards Deanie.

"And if I can get a chance to talk to Professor Dedu—why not?"

"Susan could've come back from her career with you," Barett said.

"I had no idea you were coming out," she said to Randall, "and, in any case, when I'm at the office I can't really schedule anything like that. I just head for Penn Station when I can and jump on the train—it's a lot easier that way."

Deanie knew that Susan went to an office near Rockefeller Center a couple of times a week to do promotional work for a publisher, but she had been under the impression that Susan was going to take the month of June off.

"You're still going in?" Deanie asked.

"Not really," she said, "I just had to tie up some loose ends today."

"And you just wanted to go for a ride with Deanie," Barett said to Randall.

"We did have a good talk," Randall said. "At least I did." He lifted his drink. "A toast to Deanie."

Susan put her hand on Deanie's shoulder. "Are your ears burning up with all that?"

"My ears are okay," she said, "but my stomach could use some attention."

Barett picked two ale bottles off the coffee table and held them up to his eyes like binoculars. "I'll give your stomach some attention," he said.

Susan turned to Deanie, ignoring Barett. "You haven't eaten. We just had some lasagne before you got here. I could heat it." She looked at Randall. "Sound all right?"

"Sounds good," Randall said.

"I'll just grab an apple or something," Deanie said.

Suddenly it seemed very quiet. Deanie could hear the barely audible scraping of the forsythia across the screens—like a thousand little hacksaws on a thousand little prison bars. She stopped and listened for—she didn't know what. But she could still hear, way off in the distance, hacksaws on prison bars.

Susan touched Deanie's arm. "Wake up." Deanie blinked and followed her into the kitchen. "Randall is staying overnight so he can meet Kojo. We've decided to have a few people over tomorrow night. I called Kojo this afternoon as soon as Barett told me that Randall was on his way," she said. "Kojo couldn't come tonight, but we thought a party tomorrow would be better anyhow. Now I've got to go kiss Gary good-night and make sure there's a bed made up for the driver."

Deanie said good-night to everyone and went out and stood by the steps breathing deeply of the fresh night air. As she looked up at the few stars that had come out, she heard Barett in the kitchen clinking ice cubes and speaking loudly to the others in the living room, his normally deep voice rumbling.

"Why don't we have a poetry reading and get some jungle music and really *do* it. And then we could—" The rest of his sentence faded as he walked away from the kitchen.

Barett had been lighting one cigarette off another and Randall and Susan had been puffing on cigarillos. The cool air with its scent of marsh water blowing from the sound felt good at first, but as she stood there hearing—not listening to—the voices inside she felt a chill, heard somebody clinking ice cubes, and went back into the kitchen.

Randall was focusing all of his attention on aiming an ice cube tray of water toward the open freezer compartment.

"I need a sweater," she said, looking among the sweaters and jackets hanging on the coat rack behind the door. She pulled out a cotton sweater and started for the living room to tell Susan she was borrowing it. Randall walked in ahead of her.

"I'm *not* helping Kojo in some *secret* revolutionary *project*," Susan said with irritation.

Deanie stopped and put on the sweater.

"If Kojo became President of Ghana and gave you a chance to become his Minister of Finance"—Barett paused—"would you, could you, turn him down?"

"You're giving me a headache," Susan said.

"I'm sorry," Barett said in a conciliatory tone, "it just seemed—" He broke off in a burst of coughing.

"Maybe Barett could be the Minister of Physical Fitness," Randall said.

"Now *there's* an idea," Susan said.

Deanie put an apple in the sweater pocket and went for the door. Barett and Randall said something at the same time and laughed.

"Susan took Kojo's course—ask her."

"A film course?" Randall asked.

"No. It was an African oral traditions course, a night class that I audited." There was still a note of irritation in Susan's voice, and Deanie went out wondering why Susan had never mentioned auditing one of Kojo's classes. But, she reflected, why should she have mentioned that? About ten yards into the early dark Deanie heard Susan's voice getting sharp and loud. "I am *not* going to get old."

"That's the spirit," Randall said.

Barett laughed and burst into a fit of coughing.

Deanie knew that Barett could have a sarcastic tongue sometimes, but tonight he seemed to really be giving Susan a hard time. She was drawing a blank as to why. She hurried towards Zerk's place. She couldn't wait to be in his arms. She looked towards the gatehouse and saw that the carpenter hadn't left the porch light on. That's all she needed—a sprained ankle, a punctured foot. The obstacle course of sawhorses, wood scraps, and boards with nails sticking up was bad enough during the day. Zerk had a flashlight she could borrow, but almost running now she hoped she wouldn't need it, that he'd be at home, that she'd be in his arms till tomorrow.

* * *

Deanie and Zerk had been lovers since May—he had moved into the stable apartment late last fall after staying with Barett and Susan for a couple of weeks. He had just taken a shot at college after coming back from Vietnam—but, as he said, he wasn't quite ready to hit the books. So, thanks to Barett, he found the apartment and moved in. Now he was operating a crane—actually two—one at the nuclear plant they were building at Shoreham and one in the woods between the Sanborn estate and the place next door where their friend Iris Nestervich lived.

The light through the doorway seemed to flicker, telling Deanie that Zerk was probably sitting in the dark watching TV. He was. She stopped at the screen door and ran her fingernail down the screen to get his attention.

"Is that a zipper?" Zerk said, getting up from the sofa. "Somebody trying to get my attention by unzipping her zipper?"

"I don't hear anything," she said, going into the living room. "I need a hug, if that'll get your attention."

"It sure will," he said. Zerk was tall and muscular and his hair brushed a couple of inches below his shoulders, and when he threw his arms out Deanie leaned into him and held on as if she were about to slip off a cliff. "Hey," he said, "you did need a hug, didn't you?"

"Umm," she sighed, rubbing her cheek on his shoulder.

"Did your tryout go all right?"

"I got the job"—she paused—"but the tryout's kind of hard to explain."

"You had to prance naked around the studio—or whatever it was?"

"Sort of—except we had to sit in a chair while we did it."

"Really?" He stood back a little and frowned.

She nodded.

37

"And there were other people trying out?"

She nodded and explained how it had gone, how she had had a flashback to her uncle's farm.

"You mean watching the model and pulling on the cord reminded you of helping a cow to give birth on your uncle's farm?"

"No—it didn't *remind* me," she said, "I was just *doing* it again for a couple of seconds."

"Well, that can happen," he said. "How do you feel now?"

She sighed and nestled her head on his shoulder. "Much better," she said.

He held her closer and slid his hand up to caress the back of her neck. "I think I know how you felt. People were certainly more congenial on the farm."

"They were." She sighed and ran her hand down his arm. "We had these big meals all the time and people were always stopping by in the evening to say hello and my uncle even taught me, a *girl*," she leaned back and rolled her eyes, "how to shoot his shotgun so I could shoot at old coffee cans with my cousins."

"Was it a 12 gauge?"

She nodded. "Yup. It was an old double-barreled goose gun."

"That's quite an accomplishment."

"Just farm fun," she said, feeling his arms tightening around her. She turned her face up to meet his kiss and after a moment stepped back, her hands on his shoulders. "Have you talked to Susan and Barett today?"

"No. Why?"

"I just felt some really strange vibrations tonight. There seemed to be a lot of tension in the air when they started talking about Kojo. Barett seemed to be bugging her on purpose."

Zerk looked thoughtful. "Barett's probably jealous. Susan knew Kojo in London before he came here. As a matter of fact, she gave his résumé to some administrative type who hired him—Arnold Moskey, chairman or dean of something—and that's how he got the job. Or"—he paused—"maybe it's a case of the 'best defense is a good offense'—I think Barett's got something going with Iris."

All of this was news to Deanie, but she was too tired and in no mood to ask Zerk for any details, even when it concerned her friend Iris. "Really?" she said. "I just," she paused, "I just can't talk any more."

She felt Zerk moving his lips along her neck to her ear. "Let's go to bed," he said, "I want to love you closer."

Deanie felt a surge of relief and stepping back she reached out and turned off the TV.

THREE

Deanie wasn't surprised the next morning when Susan called to tell her that the party where Randall could meet Kojo was now going to be held at Iris's house. Iris, a would-be school teacher in her early twenties, had rented the house on the adjoining estate about a year ago. She and her housemate Terence, a fellow who taught at the community college, had a lot of parties, and people often came to read poems or play their own music. The parties always seemed to be crowded and lively. Iris, who tended bar and waitressed at the Shamrock Tavern, kept the crowd level up by constantly telling lonely patrons to "stop by sometime." And when she was working as a substitute teacher she invited almost everyone in sight. And so if you wanted a big party on short notice, with maybe some singing and poetry reading—and that's what Randall had wanted, and Susan had promised—you called Iris. Deanie had told Susan she'd watch Gary while Barett did some shopping for the party, and now, she realized, it was time to get going. She put her teacup in the sink, wiped some sugar off the counter, picked up her bag, and went out.

Outside it was a beautiful green day with a refreshing breeze blowing through the trees as Deanie stood by the drive, as she often did, waiting for Barett to pick her up. She was watching the carpenter, a man in his late fifties or early sixties, show his new helper where to cut some boards with a circular saw. The helper was about her age, lean and blond, with sharp hazel eyes. The strings of his nail apron were tied in a big bow that rested on his bare back, just above his belt. From time to time he moved a board, glanced at her, and reached for another. Something about what he was doing, building something, while she stood there and merely watched brought on a brief wave of anxiety, and as he cradled the cut boards in his arms and carried them inside the house she wondered when she'd be seeing the land of her dreams. She'd had her heart set on going to Naples for so long that she could hardly wait to get there.

While she waited she whispered words from a song that had sprung to mind as she watched a couple of sea gulls rising and dropping in the wind. The words were from the old Army Air Corps song, one of the many recordings that she and her father used to play and sing a line or two from when they went through his collection of big band records on Sunday afternoons ("Off we go—in to the wild blue yonder, Climbing high—into the sun..."). But that was years ago and those were the only words she had remembered and without realizing it she had moved on to another song, and when the carpenter's helper came back out she was lingering on Otis Redding's "(Sittin' on) The Dock of the Bay" ("watchin' the tide roll away...can't do what ten people tell me to do...").

She looked up the drive. Barett still wasn't in sight. The sea gulls cried to the wind and floated across the field towards the treetops that seemed to outline a doorway into the sky, and she felt drawn to it, as if with the right word or combination of words she could soar to it and pass through to the other side beyond the atmosphere. Suddenly she was reminded that Otis Redding had died in a plane crash and it struck her that there was some syllogism struggling to be born from her remembrances of a few moments before. Certain words from the old song and the Sunday afternoons and the Otis Redding song kept running through her mind—in the same order, but repeating themselves with different spacing or emphases—she couldn't tell which— "wild... blue... high... father... promise... can't... wildblue... high-father... promisecan't... can'twild... bluehigh... fatherpromise..." It was like a roulette wheel or like being an arrow spinning inside a circle of words and then stopping on one. You could land on "wild" or "promise" or "can't." But she wondered how you landed on any word in particular. Did you choose it? Or did it choose you? She would stop on "blue" because she was looking at a blue doorway into the sky. Or maybe she would stop on "promise" because of what she expected at the end of the summer. She was still circling around the ring of words when she heard Barett's station wagon coming down the drive from the mansion and found herself watching the muscles moving on the helper's shoulders.

He was good-looking all right. Their eyes met and she smiled and he nodded and turned back to his work. And as she looked back towards the drive the thought crossed her mind that he was bashful. How touching, she thought, and she looked back to see him pushing a wheelbarrow towards the house, the muscles on his shoulders glistening with sweat.

For reasons known only to himself Barett always, as far as she knew, drove well under the speed limit. Off the road he barely moved. Now as the breeze rustled the leaves and rippled the long grass between the woods and the drive, Barett's station wagon floated towards her, a brown raft on a sea of green.

Deanie reached for the back door and, seeing the seat covered with boxes of old newspapers and empty bottles, sat in front next to Gary and, closing the door, saw the carpenter's helper watching her.

"Hi, Deanie," Barett said. He was wearing his sunglasses, his shades, as they often called them.

"Hello," she said. "And how are you, Gary?"

He shrugged slowly, nearly touching his shoulders to his ears.

"You don't know?" Barett asked. He shrugged again and fidgeted with his seat belt buckle. "Can't you answer Deanie?"

"It's okay," she said.

"He could answer you."

"It's okay."

"I'm really tired," Barett said. His husky voice was lower than usual. He sounded like he was speaking through a cardboard cylinder from a roll of toilet paper.

"Where's Randall?" Deanie asked.

"He's taking a nap." Barett sighed and reached for a cigarette from among the five or six open packages spread along the top of the dashboard.

It didn't look like Barett and Gary were going to be very talkative.

* * *

Barett had forgotten his checkbook so he had to stop by his office to get it. The Peeze campus was fairly new, dating from the middle fifties when John Quincy Hunningfer Peeze gave a money-losing eighteen-hole golf course and an adjoining unfinished shopping center to the state of New York for "the establishment of a center of useful higher education for local citizens."

Mr. Peeze, a native Long Islander who had spent sixty of his ninety years making a fortune in lead and zinc, died shortly after the dedication ceremonies when the remodeled shopping center was put into service as a student center, three lecture halls, an infirmary, a maintenance shop, and twenty-two classrooms.

The golf course clubhouse had been converted into a dormitory, and the pro shop had become the administration building.

Until they started building dormitories on the new campus, Peeze Point had been little more than a couple of stores, a post office, and a fire station on a patchwork stretch of scrub oak, mountain laurel, pignut hickory, sassafras, chokecherry, dogwood, maple, and pine woods between Port Jefferson and Shoreham on the north shore of Long Island. Now you could see signs of growth—a couple of new traffic lights, a Jack-in-the-Box restaurant, a coin-operated laundry. And there was noticeably more traffic during the regular school year when the more than ten thousand students were around.

As they pulled onto the campus Deanie couldn't see anyone—except a couple playing tennis. As they passed by the graduate dorm where Kojo had an apartment, she saw Kojo's teaching assistant, and three other guys shooting baskets on the court alongside the building. She had met him at Kojo's apartment after one of her classes. He seemed rather withdrawn at times, but at other times he was full of energy and in tune exactly with what she was feeling. More than once she had sat in the library, watching him grading papers, wondering what it would be like to really spend some time with him.

*   *   *

As they approached the basketball court on their way back to the shopping center Deanie saw that Kojo's teaching assistant was the only player left. He was holding the basketball under his arm and talking to a black woman who looked to be in her mid-twenties. He was wearing faded jeans and a blue T-shirt darkened with sweat. His usually light complexion was red from exertion. The black woman wore a blue sack dress. They both waved.

Barett lifted his hand from the wheel in acknowledgement.

"Who is she?" Deanie asked.

"Kojo's R.A." Barett said.

"I didn't know he had a research assistant."

Barett pulled at his beard. "No." He laughed lightly and coughed. "I'm sorry, Deanie." He coughed again. "By 'R.A.' I meant 'resident admirer.' Her name's Linda."

Deanie looked back to the court. The woman was naked, her swollen belly was huge. Was she pregnant with twins? Had she swallowed the basketball? Where was the basketball? Suddenly the guy stretched his hands all the way to the basket rim, tore it off, whirled around and began chasing the woman around and around the court. Deanie gasped, turned to Barett, and saw Gary hanging by his neck from a seat belt attached to the dome light. She gasped again and covered her face with her hands.

"What's wrong?" Barett said.

"They can't breathe. Nobody can breathe," she said.

Barett stopped the station wagon. "What do you mean?"

Deanie uncovered her face. Gary was sitting in the seat, scowling at her. The woman on the court was dressed and holding the basketball. The fellow with her was jumping at the basket rim, trying to slap free the tangled net.

"I'm not sure. I felt like nobody could breathe."

*   *   *

The sun was setting as Deanie cut through the scrub oak and scattered pines heavy with violet evening shadow. Zerk had left a note on his door telling her to stop by his crane that was parked in the clearing along the path to Iris's house. The bridle path that ran from the Sanborn estate through the woods and across the abandoned pasture to the next estate was cool and quiet and Deanie was enjoying the peace and quiet after the shopping trip with Barett and Gary.

Straight ahead a spotlight swept dimly through the trees. At first the crane and bulldozer across the clearing looked like Tonka toys in the evening light. A diesel engine coughed and roared. That's the real thing, she thought. "The real thing."

As soon as Deanie said that she remembered Randall's saying that the model's orgasm was "the real thing" and for a moment she saw herself and the other models struggling in a pool of heavy water. The machine coughed and roared and she envisioned Zerk settled in the front of it, manipulating the controls. Gradually the roars settled into a steady rumble as she continued along the path through the trees.

Zerk had made a dump site for tank trucks where he dug and backfilled huge holes with the truck-mounted crane and a bulldozer that he had gotten from his brother's construction company in Queens. She didn't know what they dumped there and she hadn't really thought about it. She knew Zerk did have a small sign at the other end of the property that said:

Shoreline Heavy Equipment
Operator Training
School
By Appointment Only

And across the row of rectangular pits in front of her, on the other side of the clearing, was a large sign facing the entrance that, she recalled, described the pits as "model basements" for "operator and carpenter training."

Across the row of four pits the crane crouched, its engine rhythmically roaring and idling, bellowing like a huge, blind animal groping for the way out of a cave. The top of its black boom sliced the sky above the trees and hung heavily over the clearing. A spotlight on the red cab swept the trees to the left of Deanie and came around to shine straight at her, and as she lifted her hand as if to shield her eyes, the light, weak in the lingering daylight, faded across the leaves and the engine quit.

"Deanie!" Zerk yelled. His voice was deep and sharp.

"Hello."

"Come on around."

Deanie followed the road Zerk was trying to light up for her, and as she rounded the second turn it began to look like the road ran in an oval all the way around the pits that for a moment in the growing darkness reminded her of pictures she'd seen of mass graves in some distant place.

Zerk playfully moved the light ahead of her, and as she came up to the crane he shut it off and jumped down.

"Hi. I shined the light for you so you wouldn't fall in a pit." He took her hand and smiled.

"That was very thoughtful of you."

"It was nothing." He kissed her hand and unrolled a pack of cigarettes from his T-shirt sleeve. His brown eyes sparkled for a moment as he held a match to the cigarette. He wore a rolled red bandanna as a headband, and his long sandy-brown hair brushed his muscular shoulders. His faded jeans and sneakers were spotted with grease. He rolled the pack of cigarettes back into his sleeve. "Let's go," he said. He blew a speck of tobacco from the tip of his tongue and brushed out the ends of his long mustache.

"Does this road go all the way around the pits?" she asked.

"Yeah. Why?"

"I just noticed that it seems to go around"—she paused—"like a little race track."

"I do a little racin' on it," he said, "but that's just inside my head when I'm really pressed for time." He sighed and blew another speck of tobacco from his tongue. "I try to keep this whole thing low-key. I just know my customers, follow my tracks, and watch out for the high-tension lines." He pointed overhead.

"I don't see anything." Now she saw them. "There they are."

"They're there all right. I hit 'em once."

"What happened?"

"I backed the boom into 'em and next thing I know there were blue arcs and sparks shooting all over the place. So I pulled ahead a couple of feet and that was that."

"Weren't you shocked or anything?"

"No. If the crane had been on metal tracks like the bulldozer it would have been a different story, but since this rig is on truck tires, as long as you stay in the cab you're okay. It's when you panic, you get in trouble. When you touch the ground it's all over. When you ground it you buy it."

"I get the picture."

"When you ground it you fry."

"I get the picture."

"When you ground it arcs and sparks shoot out your ass."

"Zerk, I get the picture."

"So after I pulled away a couple of feet I just sat there and had a cigarette and it wasn't—I don't know—ten or fifteen minutes before a couple of guys from the power company came tearin' in here with their little amber light about to fly off the top of their truck." He pointed his finger up and made a spiraling motion. "Then the cops came. Then the people from across the street came over to see what was going on."

"How did they get here so fast?"

"They've got gauges and maps at the substations that show power drains and where they are. Then they just get on their radio, and if a crew is in the neighborhood it doesn't take 'em too long to find the trouble."

"What finally happened?"

"Nothing. It was my first day here with the crane and I was just parking it. I hadn't done any digging yet. Nobody asked any questions."

The clearing along the path widened as they got closer to the house, and gradually it curved around a tall stand of pines, and now the lit-up house was right ahead of them, and Deanie could see Iris in the yard.

"You made it," Iris yelled. She was standing in the light from a floodlight fastened to the side of the house and holding her growling white boxer by the collar. She was wearing a white motorcycle helmet, a pink sleeveless top, jeans, and sneakers.

"Of course we made it," Zerk said. "Could've made it blindfolded." He jumped into a karate stance and the dog snapped at a large moth.

"Albert!" Iris shouted. "Sit down." The dog sat and she fastened a leash to his collar. The leash ran to a rusty iron clothesline post by the corner of the house.

Iris pulled off the helmet and handed it to Zerk. He straightened up, and as she flipped her long blond hair away from her neck she seemed to stretch a little taller than Zerk.

"Hi, Deanie," she said, as she brushed her long eyelashes up with the tips of her fingers. She pulled back her thin, plucked eyebrows and massaged her temples for a moment. "That helmet makes my head itch." Her hazel-brown eyes were big and she wore her green eye shadow well. Her lips were thin, as if drawn with red pencil. When she smiled her face became a czarist poem and her large nose curtsied. She rested her hands flat on her hips, her elbows pointing out, and leaned towards them. "Just a second while I cover my bike." Iris pulled a dark green tarp off the porch and carried it back to the red motorcycle that rested against the garage. The dog followed her, his bobbed tail erect, his uncut ears flopping over the tall grass. Deanie noticed that since her last visit somebody had put up a basketball goal over the garage door.

The two-story white-clapboard house, Deanie knew from an inscribed antique picture hanging in the dining room, was built by a Civil War veteran, a colonel, in the late 1860's. She liked the porch that ran all the way along the side and then clear across the front of the house. In the past month or so she had sat out there a few times, relaxing with Zerk and Iris's housemate Terence, listening to him play his guitar and sing cowboy songs. The cowboy songs were a little boring after the first two or three, but she didn't let it bother her because Terence was so sincere. And in any case, Zerk always put on a tape of The Eagles or America or The Moody Blues after Terence had sung three or four songs.

49

Iris went up the steps and led them into the kitchen. The walls were blue, the cupboards were blue, the counter tops and linoleum floor were blue, somebody had even painted the refrigerator blue, and a blue lightbulb shone over the sink.

Zerk hung the helmet behind the door and opened the refrigerator.

"Just make yourselves at home," Iris said. "I'm going to change the bulb so people can see what they're doing. Last time I left the blue bulb in, and when everybody left, this place was a mess."

The large living room had three slip-covered sofas, several stuffed chairs, and an upright piano pushed against the faded tan and magenta flowered wallpaper. Across the gray rug several cigarette burns led to a standing metal ashtray by the new yellow drapes that seemed to push the high cream-colored ceiling even higher. All of the long narrow windows had new yellow drapes. Deanie sat on a sofa where she could see people coming into the kitchen. Zerk sat next to her.

"Your new drapes really cheer the place up," Deanie said.

"I had to do something," Iris said. "Terence is such a gloomy bastard."

"Thanks a lot," Terence said, coming into the kitchen with a bag of groceries. Deanie figured Iris's remark was meant for him to hear. He was, as usual, wearing a western outfit—a western hat, a red-plaid shirt, a leather vest, jeans, and pointed western boots. He mumbled something and asked Iris where she had put the bowls for the potato chips. As he moved around the kitchen his thick brown hair and curled handlebar mustache made him look really together, Deanie thought. Yet something about his ruddy cheeks and darting brown eyes sometimes made him look as if he was on the verge of coming unglued.

Terence came into the living room. "Good to see you tonight," he said.

"Thanks," Deanie said.

"Hello," Zerk said, getting up. "Either of you want a beer?" He went into the kitchen.

"I'm going to get some wine," Deanie said.

"No thanks," Terence said, "I've got a drink around here someplace."

"Are you going to play or read anything?" Deanie asked.

"I'll see what happens. A friend of mine might bring his banjo. Maybe we'll do somethin'," he said, turning for the kitchen. "I have to go get a bag of ice."

Iris came into the room carrying a large upright tape recorder, and Zerk followed her and moved a table lamp to make room. Iris thanked him and he smiled and sat next to Deanie with his beer. Iris plugged in the recorder, adjusted the reels, and started it on low volume playing some Eric Clapton. Deanie and Zerk watched her walk back towards the hallway to the bedrooms.

"Are Barett and Susan both coming?" Zerk asked.

"Yes," she said. "And so is Randall."

"Should be interesting."

"Do really think Barett and Iris are having an affair?"

"Oh, it seems like it, but it's not the kind of thing I'd worry about unless..."

"Unless what?"

"Unless Susan and Kojo have something going and then— anything could happen."

"I'd have a lot of trouble believing that," Deanie said. "I don't need anything like that on my mind now—I just want to do what I have to do and get to Naples at the end of the summer."

*   *   *

By eleven o'clock the place was packed, and, Deanie hoped, the troublemakers and cops had come and gone for the evening. Around nine-thirty Iris had thrown out two high school kids for lighting up a hash pipe in the kitchen, and not ten minutes later two Suffolk County cops had come to the door to get Arnold Moskey, the Dean of the Graduate School, to move his big

Cadillac from where he had parked it on the side of the narrow blacktop road in front of the house.

"What'd I tell ya?" Iris had said loudly to everybody in the kitchen. "Ten minutes earlier and we'd all be up the creek with paddles." She sidled into the living room and stood squinting into the upper corners of the room as if she had forgotten something. "You can't be too careful."

"You can say that again," Zerk had said, shaking his fists mockingly.

"They got some nerve, those guys," Iris had said.

"Rotten kids," somebody had yelled.

Then Iris had pushed her hair back from her face and turned away through the crowd.

As people moved from in front of her Deanie saw Carl Peterson, the Shakespeare scholar, sitting in the stuffed chair across from her and Zerk, and she realized that he was the one who had shouted "rotten kids." He was wearing Terence's western hat and holding a glass of whiskey on the arm of the chair. He had been talking about "the last good war" and how he had made it through Normandy in the summer of 1944—when Iris came in. Now he was quiet and appeared to be in a trance.

*   *   *

Deanie had been moving around, talking to people, and as far as she could tell, Zerk had been keeping to himself, except to give people a hand. He'd fixed Iris's tape recorder when the reel had stuck, and he'd helped Terence tap a keg of beer, and he'd gone out to help Barett and Randall carry in the vodka, wine, and food from Barett's station wagon. When it started to get smoky he propped open some windows.

A guy and a girl came into the living room with amplifiers and speakers for a bass and a guitar, and Deanie went out on the porch to see what was going on. Susan and Randall were standing in the yard, talking and smoking, both wearing jeans and cotton sweaters. Deanie stood back to let two guys bump past her with cymbals, stands, and drums. One dropped a cow bell that clanked down the steps. She picked it up for him and then went to join Susan and Randall. A haze of bugs and moths vibrated around the yard light. Albert had circled the clothesline post snapping at passing moths and winding his leash till he had only a few inches left between his collar and the post. Deanie saw a look of perplexity in his wrinkled face as he stood there staring at the post, his tongue hanging out.

"You look as perplexed as Albert," Deanie said.

"Albert who?" Randall asked.

"The dog."

Randall looked towards Albert. "He's a mean lookin' son-of-a-bitch."

"That's what you get from having too short a leash," Arnold Moskey said.

"You startled me," Susan said.

Deanie hadn't noticed him come up either. He was smoking a long-stemmed pipe and the reflected yard light on his glasses hid his eyes. He wore a powder-blue sport coat and a dark-blue tie, and his white hair was cut short, reducing the starkness of the hairline around his balding crown.

"As your leash is shortened, the more likely you are to get mean-looking." His voice was high-pitched and gentle. "The problem is that many people shorten their own leashes whether they know it or not." He smiled and puffed on his pipe.

They all looked towards the dog who was still staring at the post. It felt like they were observing an official moment of silence—as she recalled witnessing during her waitressing days at the Elks' club and the V.F.W. hall at home. The musicians began warming up, and the moment of silence was over.

Randall held up his arm and seemed to make a show of sliding his sleeve back and looking at his watch. "Has anybody heard from Professor Dedu? It's after eleven."

Susan shrugged and looked at Deanie. "Have you seen him?"

"I haven't seen him," she said. The music was louder now and had gone beyond the warm-up stage. Deanie took a couple of side-steps towards the house and the others followed. Behind her she heard Susan introducing Randall to the dean. She turned to let Susan catch up to her. "Who's sitting with Gary?"

"Randall's driver."

"I would've thought he'd be here wearing a lampshade."

"He just wanted to sit and watch TV. And that was fine with me."

At the end of the living room by the hallway that led to the bedrooms three guys were playing electric piano, electric bass, and drums, and a girl was playing an electric guitar. They were playing "Greensleeves"—a little loud for a ballad, but not bad, Deanie thought. She couldn't see them all at once. She was halfway through the kitchen where her momentum had been stopped by the people crowding the doorway. Randall, Susan, and Arnold Moskey were behind her. As she leaned from one side to the other to see the musicians she saw Zerk, still on the sofa. He spotted her and raised his eyebrows in recognition. She hadn't been looking for Barett, but she noticed that he wasn't in sight and neither was Iris.

* * *

"It's midnight and still no Kojo," Randall said to Susan. "Why don't you try to call him?" They were sitting on the sofa next to Deanie and Zerk.

"I'll try," she said, "but I'm sure he'll be here."

"There's a phone in the bedroom," Deanie said. "It's probably quieter back there."

"All right." She held her cigarillo over her head to avoid burning anybody and went away through the crowd.

Deanie watched Susan till she vanished into the hallway. She was wondering if Susan was wondering where Barett and Iris were. Suddenly Iris appeared from the hallway and came over and stood by them.

"How ya doin'?" she asked, a little out of breath.

"Fine," Deanie said.

"I was in the bedroom showing Barett some of my art work. Susan came in sayin' she's trying to get hold of Kojo."

Deanie saw Barett come out of the hallway and head into the kitchen.

"What kind of art work?" Randall asked.

"Some charcoal sketches and some oil paintings. There's one of my paintings behind you."

The three of them turned around. Deanie knew the picture. It was a realistic oil painting, about three feet square, of a jug of Clorox bleach and a jar of Vaseline petroleum jelly on an orange background.

Randall squinted at it, glanced at Iris, and looked back. "Striking," he said. "Those colors really press against each other, make it work."

"Yeah?" Iris said. "Ya think so?"

"Yeah."

"That's my favorite painting. I spent a whole semester on it and it's the best one in my portfolio."

"It's certainly focused."

"It's getting back to the object."

"Yeah. Getting back to the object," Randall said, as Iris sat down between him and Deanie.

"This beer can is an empty object," Zerk said, holding a can out and crushing it.

*   *   *

The band had stopped playing and Terence and four others were standing where the musicians had been. They were apparently discussing their poems and song lyrics and trying to decide who was going to read or sing what. Randall and Iris were discussing "objects" and Zerk seemed to be withdrawing into himself.

"Do you feel okay?" Deanie asked.

He put his hand on her thigh. "I don't feel as good as *you* do, but," he shrugged, "I'm okay." He nodded towards the corner. "Those three over there look like they're having quite a time."

"They do," she agreed. Three people were on a stuffed chair, one in the seat, one on each arm, and they were laughing hysterically, bumping foreheads. "The woman in the seat teaches behavioral psychology and that's her lover on her left. She's a grad student in psych. The man on her right teaches political science and races model airplanes. He and his wife are getting divorced. That's his wife standing next to you."

Pressing in on Zerk's space was the wide rear end of a blue-denim, wrap-around skirt. Just as he looked to his right a pale hand with long red nails belonging to the owner of the skirt slid around the denim and disappeared under the flap to flutter it in a frantic dig for an itch. He looked back at Deanie, rolled his eyes, and took a drink.

* * *

Now Susan was back, sitting on the coffee table, telling Randall that Kojo had been tied up with some friends from the U.N. who had come out to visit him, and that they were all on their way to the party. Terence was trying to read a poem above the noise.

"Let's have some quiet for the cowboy poet," Zerk said.

This seemed to wake Carl Peterson from his trance. "Hit 'em again!" he bellowed.

Zerk shouted again and laughed and saluted Terence and, as the noise level dropped, leaned back to listen.

"This is called 'The Late News,'" Terence said, "as in the late news on TV."

"This is more like it," Randall said. "I wish Kojo would hurry up." He took a drink. "Is he always late?" He looked at Deanie.

She shrugged and sipped her wine.

"'The Late News,'" Terence repeated—
   "What standing does a sorcerer have before the law?
   That was the question being puzzled over today by
   county authorities.
   Early this morning, seventeen local residents
   complained to the county prosecutor's office
   that they are under a sorcerer's curse
   that has already driven scores of local youths mad.
   The residents said that the alleged sorcerer
    arrived late yesterday aboard *Air Force One*,
   entered a waiting limousine of unidentified origin, and
   sped to the city cemetery
   where he cursed everybody in town
   when several passers-by prevented him from digging up
   the city's only returned fatality of the war.
   The alleged sorcerer did not say why he wanted the
   body,
   and furthermore, only the county coroner's office can
   grant
   a permit to disinter corpses,
   the county authorities said.
   The alleged sorcerer gave them three days to change
   their minds, they charged—warning that otherwise, 'You
   will fall into my power, one after the other,
   one of you every day.'
   The weather for tomor—"
He stopped reading and stared into space.
"Is that all?" Susan asked.
"The broadcast was cut off," Randall said, "by the *power*."
He made a spooky gesture with his hands in front of his face.
"I see." Susan nodded and took a sip of her drink.
   Now a guy with curly brown hair and a denim vest over a T-
shirt was strumming a guitar and singing in what sounded to
Deanie like a midwestern twang—

"Hey, Mister Nixon,
   What are you gonna dooo?
   Hey, Mister Nixon,
   What are you gonna dooo?
   I got a horse that's ready
   And a gun that's steady tooo,
   But I ain't gonna kill no Congs for yooou,
   But I ain't—"

There was a quick movement past her and Zerk had one hand on the singer's shoulder and one on the guitar. The singer pushed towards Zerk and Zerk pushed back saying something through clenched teeth. The singer's face flushed, he nodded, and Zerk let go of him.

"Must have struck a nerve," Deanie said.

"I guess so," Susan said.

Now Zerk put his arm around the singer's shoulders and they went out.

Deanie saw that nobody seemed to pay any attention to the way Zerk had stopped the song. No, Iris had. Iris looked startled, and she was staring in the direction that Zerk and the singer had gone. Now somebody else was reading something and the singer came back in with a beer and sat on the piano bench.

Iris looked relieved. Zerk came in with a beer and stood back against the wall.

"Is Zerk okay?" Iris asked.

"He looks okay," Deanie said. She leaned closer to Iris. "He's been having nightmares about his time in Vietnam." She paused. "He woke up screaming the other night," she said. "But he calmed down in a few minutes and went back to sleep."

"If Terence had known," Iris said, "he wouldn't have read that poem. The poem and the song were probably a little too much tonight."

Deanie looked back towards Zerk. He was gone. "I'm going to get some more ice," she said. Iris moved to let her up and she made her way to the kitchen and went outside wondering if Zerk was all right.

*   *   *

Deanie was walking in the shadows when she saw Zerk come around the back corner of the house. Looking towards her, he appeared to catch his breath as if he was up to something.

"Hello," he said.

"Hi, Zerk."

Zerk stood for a moment by the corner of the house. He looked from Deanie to Albert and back to her.

"I'm wonderin' if you could help me out?"

"How?" she said, studying his face. He looked okay.

"Well," he said, pausing to scratch his head, "I need somebody to go into the bathroom, lock the door, and open the window for me." He pointed to the window that faced the side porch.

"How come?"

"Well—" He put his hand up to cover a belch. "Albert and I have a little performance for everybody and we need a makeup room."

"And?"

"And it needs the element of surprise," Zerk said. "Okay?"

"Okay," she said. She started for the house, feeling good that they were alone and doing something together.

*   *   *

As soon as Deanie opened the window Zerk's foot came through, followed by his leg, and his elbow, and now Albert came sliding over the sill and down Zerk's leg. Zerk kept hold of Albert's collar while he squeezed his head under the window and pulled his other leg through. Still holding onto the collar, he stepped over and sat on the edge of the tub. "He must weigh fifty pounds," Zerk said. Deanie shut the window and closed the curtains. "Thanks," he said.

Somebody rattled the doorknob, and Deanie cupped her hands over her nose and mouth to disguise her voice. "Use the bathroom upstairs."

"That's the spirit," Zerk said. He stroked the dog's head. "Okay, there's a can of shaving cream under the sink. Could you get it out?"

She handed him the aerosol can and he set it on the edge of the tub. Suddenly Albert tried to pull away and his churning feet threw the rug behind him and his toenails clicked on the tiles like spilling BB's.

"Take it easy, Albert." Zerk patted his shoulder and rubbed his heaving chest. "Take it easy." He snorted and settled down and yawned.

"What a mouth," Deanie said. "He could have a whole grapefruit in there and you wouldn't even know it."

"But he wouldn't hurt a flea. Would you, Albert?" Zerk patted his back, and the dog's rear end wiggled. "Now I need some shaving lotion—it's in the medicine chest."

She gave him the lotion.

"Okay," Zerk said. He moved around the dog, holding the collar with his left hand, and knelt facing the dog's left side. He lined up the dog and aimed him towards the door. "Okay. Now stand behind the door and when I say 'Open it' pull it all the way open and then let go of it when he takes off."

She moved to Zerk's left, stood back against the wall, and leaned out to grasp the doorknob with both hands. She still wasn't sure what he was doing.

Zerk set the bottle of shaving lotion on the floor between his knees and screwed off the cap with his right hand. He reached across the dog and picked up the can of shaving cream. He shook it, and the dog strained forward, snorted, and looked back at Zerk.

"Are you ready?"

"That's not going to hurt him, is it?"

"No. He'll wipe it off. It'll evaporate. Don't worry. Ready?"

She nodded.

"Anybody by the door?"

She cracked the door and peeked out. "No."

"Okay. Now lean back and hold onto the doorknob." As Zerk started spraying the puffy mass of white foam around the dog's snout he shook his head and strained for the door. "Take it easy. Good boy. Take it easy. Good boy."

The veins in Zerk's left arm stood out like cord as he gripped the collar and finished with the shaving cream. He slid the can out of the way and picked up the bottle of lotion with his right hand, tipped some lotion into his palm, set the bottle behind him, and in one sweeping motion brought his hand around to splash some lotion under the dog's tail and push him towards the door.

"Open it!" She jerked the door open and Zerk followed the dog to the doorway on his hands and knees. "Mad dog! Rabies! Mad dog! Needles in your bellybuttons!" he shouted in a high-pitched disguised voice, slammed the door, locked it, grabbed her hand, and shut off the light. "Let's get out of here."

Before they got the window up she could hear barking and screams and breaking glass. "What have we done?"

"I think they call it 'found poetry,'" he said, holding her hand and pulling her along the porch towards the back of the house. Albert was still barking and the house groaned and creaked with the shouting and screams inside.

As they passed a bedroom window the light went on and half a dozen people ran in to escape the dog. Zerk stopped by the next window and they saw two of the people scrambling for the closet door and they pulled it open and there was Barett standing with his pants down to his ankles and Iris in front of him sitting sidesaddle on a rocking horse. In an attempt to cover Barett's nakedness Iris had apparently picked up the first thing her hand had fallen on—a baseball glove.

She pulled Zerk's hand. "Don't stare," she said, "come on."

They ran to the end of the porch and jumped off and Zerk doubled over in laughter so intense that he could only wheeze.

Deanie circled back to the picnic table and sat watching them all spilling out of the doors and down the steps.

"You really did it," she said, as Zerk came towards her, throwing his arms out as if beholding a wonder.

Deanie watched them coming down, the shifting planes of light and color. They looked as though they were coming out of a painting by Duchamps. "Peezean descending a staircase," she said, a little surprised by her description.

"That's it!" Zerk shouted. He was laughing again. He twisted back and forth swinging his outstretched arms as if to indicate a vast region. "'Peezean descending a staircase.' That's it! That's it!"

* * *

The only ones in the yard now were Deanie, Zerk, Susan, Barett, and Randall. Deanie thought they were probably the last ones to be leaving, but there were still two cars in the driveway near Barett's station wagon, and there was always the chance that somebody was asleep in an obscure corner of the house or passed out behind a bush.

Once everybody had made it to the yard they all began to realize that the rabid dog scare had been a trick. Some people hadn't been fooled, but that hadn't kept them from the rush to get out. And when the political scientist sniffed some of the foam that had brushed onto his pants, the hoax was over. After that just about everybody went home.

Zerk had put Albert back on his leash, and again he had wound it up on the post. Nobody had been hurt—as far as she knew. A tipped-over cymbal had gone through the snare drum, a tray of glasses had been broken in the sink, and somebody had thrown a tray of cold cuts at the dog in an attempt to divert him. But that was about it for damage—physical damage.

Susan hadn't caught Barett and Iris in the closet, but half a dozen other people had. It was anybody's guess as to what would come of that. Iris and Terence were inside cleaning up. The way it looked to Deanie nobody but she and Zerk knew who had sent the dog into the party.

Deanie, Zerk, and Susan were sitting at the picnic table, and Barett was standing a little way off with a can of beer, sliding his foot in a little circle in the grass. He was probably trying to come up with a good story to explain what he and Iris had been doing in the closet. Randall was resting one foot on the bench and his gestures and comments ("Send him a fuckin' watch for his birthday") let everybody know how upset he was that Kojo hadn't shown up.

Somebody came out of the house. It was Carl Peterson. He walked into the shadows by the front porch and they heard him pissing on the leaves. He came across the yard towards the cars. He saw them and stopped. "Where in the hell is everybody?"

"They went home," Randall said.

"Party poopers," he said, leaning towards his car.

When he turned on his headlights, a head popped up in the car in front of his. As he pulled away, somebody got out of the other car and walked haltingly towards them. It was Kojo's teaching assistant. He looked drunk.

"What time is it?" he asked. His voice was low and sounded like a thin wooden hull running aground.

"One thirty-two," Randall said.

"Shit."

"What's the matter?" Susan asked.

"I musta fallen asleep."

"What's wrong?" Susan asked.

"Has Kojo got here yet?"

"No," she said. "Isn't he coming?" She sounded worried.

"He's supposed to—" He stumbled backwards, catching himself on Barett. "Sorry, Barett." He steadied himself. "What time did you say it was?"

"One thirty-three," Randall said.

"Damnit."

"What's the matter?" Susan asked.

"I think I was supposed to pick him up."

"I called him," Susan said, "and he told me that some friends from the U.N. were going to give him a ride. Don't worry about it."

"Shit." He sat down in the grass in front of Barett and bent over, sobbing.

Deanie went over to him, got down beside him, and put her hand on his shoulder. He was trembling. He looked frightfully vulnerable. "Can I do something?"

He didn't answer. A tear ran across his nose, and there was something in his mustache that looked like cottage cheese.

*   *   *

Deanie and Zerk decided to drive the teaching assistant back to Zerk's place for the night. They helped him into the back seat of his car and Deanie followed him in and Zerk got behind the wheel. Barett went inside the house to get him a cup of coffee.

Now Barett was coming back and Iris and Terence were with him. Susan and Randall joined them by the car. Deanie took the coffee from Barett. Kojo's teaching assistant appeared to be asleep.

"Who sent the dog in?" Randall asked.

"I don't know," Iris said. "It was probably those high school kids I threw out. I'll burn that bridge when I get to it. I've got to fix my painting before I do anything else." She sniffled and covered her face with her hands. "Or else do another one."

Deanie felt sick. She was afraid to ask her what had happened to her painting. Shit, she said to herself, what did I do now?

"What happened?" Zerk asked.

"My best painting got punched over a lamp." Iris paused and wiped tears from her cheeks. "Now it's got a hole in it the size of a toilet seat."

Deanie glanced at Zerk and sighed. She felt awful.

Headlights glared up the driveway and a long quiet car rolled past, made a U-turn, and came back to stop next to them. It was a black Cadillac with New York diplomatic plates. Susan walked over to the passenger side. The window was open. She leaned over and exchanged a few words with somebody.

"Randall," Susan said, "I want you to meet Kojo Dedu."

Randall mumbled something and went to her side. Kojo reached out and they shook hands.

"How do you do?" Kojo said. His voice was deep and had a slight British accent.

"Fine, thank you, and you?" Randall said. Deanie marvelled at his politeness after being so upset.

"Fine," Kojo said. "Susan tells me that you're interested in the comparative study of culture."

"Well," he paused, hitching up his pants. "I try to keep up with things."

"So do I," Kojo said. "Why don't we get together sometime? Susan, could you set up something for us—the three of us? We can compare notes, have a drink."

"I'll see what I can do."

"Great. We must be off now. We have an important meeting in the city. Nice to meet you, Randall."

"Good luck," Randall said.

The car rolled back down the driveway and they were gone.

Randall kicked a plastic cup across the grass and walked towards the station wagon with Barett and Susan following him. Iris and Terence went towards the house, Iris with her hands thrust into the rear pockets of her jeans.

At the porch she stopped with her foot on the bottom step and turned to them. "Good night."

"Night," Randall said.

"Thanks again," Susan said. "Too bad about your painting."

Deanie waved and Zerk started the car. As they rolled down the driveway she felt sick about the painting and she could hardly believe that the guy flopped over next to her was the same handsome guy she'd stared at in the library. Hearing his noisy breathing she recalled her vision of him on the basketball court...going around in circles...can't breathe...nobody can breathe. She puffed her breath on the car window and wiped the moisture off with her finger. I can breathe, she told herself, up to a point. She rested her head back in the seat and told herself she'd never get drawn into something like that again.

FOUR

"Working today?" Maria asked.

Deanie nodded as she finished swallowing the cheese Danish she'd picked up at a deli on her walk from the subway to Burkhart Modeltronics. She let Maria push the elevator button. She liked Maria, but right now she didn't feel like talking. She'd seen Zerk's former girlfriend's car parked in front of his place this morning and that had put a strain on her capacity for small talk. She knew that it was just a car and that it was just there and if anything had been going on the car certainly wouldn't have been there in plain sight. Still, she didn't need to see that this morning. So after getting Susan's car she had stopped at her place and run in and called Zerk.

"Hello," he had said.

"Hello," she had said. "Hello. Hello. Did you just try to call me?"

"No."

"Oh. I thought I heard my phone ringing and I didn't get to it in time. I thought maybe it was you."

"Wasn't me."

"Okay. Well, I don't want to miss my train."

"Are you okay?"

"I'm okay. What are you doing today?"

"Not much," he said. "This person I used to go out with happened to be passing through and she wants to go out for breakfast and, I don't know, talk about life's changes or something. Nothing to worry about."

"What would I worry about?"

"I don't know. I just don't want you to get the wrong idea."

"You can do whatever you want," she said, pausing, "but if there's a wrong idea, I won't get it. I've got to go now."

"See you tonight."

"Okay. Bye."

"Bye."

Inside the elevator Deanie reflected that, because July was half over, this would be her last modeling session till August. "It won't be long," Deanie said.

"What won't be long?" Maria said.

"Working here," Deanie said. "I've only got three more sessions."

"Really?"

"Two in August and one in September."

"And then you're off to Naples?"

Deanie nodded.

"Are you excited?"

"Some days more than others. But I've been so busy. Sometimes the excitement of going gets pushed into the background."

"You'll probably feel different when summer school's over."

"I think so." She smiled and flipped her hair over her shoulders.

When the doors opened the security guard looked up from a newspaper on his desk. "Hello," he said. He tipped his head to see Maria who was right behind her. "Is Teresa coming in today?"

"I don't know," Maria said. "Maybe this afternoon."

"When is the session over?" he asked.

"Around one," Maria said.

Deanie looked at the clock on the wall. It was five minutes to ten. "See you inside, Maria." She adjusted the shoulder strap of her bag, pulled out the sleeve of her Mickey Mouse T-shirt and headed for the reception area.

*   *   *

Deanie walked into the modeling area wearing a bright blue ski jacket. Teresa waved from her desk chair and Deanie smiled. She looked really cheerful, Deanie thought. Earlier Randall had said hello to her, and then he went someplace while the woman photographer gave instructions to her and the other models. Now she could see Randall across the room talking to one of his secretaries. She hoped he'd stay there or in his office while she was modeling. She didn't want to hear any bullshit from him today.

"Okay, Deanie," the photographer said, "put on your winter face and let's go over to the snow set."

Deanie moved in front of the white backdrop and stood by a pair of skis propped against an artificial pile of snow. Now she was following the photographer's directions and from the corner of her eye she saw Maria in a long leather coat and high leather boots waiting her turn. She was glad the air conditioning worked.

All through the session, through her posing with a variety of turtlenecks and ski pants, Randall sat on the edge of the photo area, with a few other people, watching the models and the photographer. As Deanie left the dressing room for the last pictures of the day, modeling fur-covered ear muffs and a coat, she saw that he was gone.

*   *   *

On the way out Deanie stopped at the receptionist's desk and tried to call Zerk, but there was no answer. She had told herself that she just wanted to say hello, though as she listened to the phone ringing she felt like a whole lot of things were trying to get said, but she couldn't say what. Now heading for the elevator, Deanie saw Randall up ahead punching out a cigarette in the ashtray on the security guard's desk.

"You did very well," Randall said.

The compliment surprised her. "Thanks," she said, stopping by the elevator.

"Are Barett and Susan picking you up?"

"No," she said, wondering how Randall knew that they were in the city. "Susan had to stop by her office, and Barett wanted to check out some bookstores."

"Are you all still meeting Kojo for lunch at the West End Cafe?"

"I'm late now," she said, hoping Randall wasn't coming. He must have talked to Susan. She turned to push the elevator button again. She didn't want to say anything, but she could feel the words already on their way out. "Are you going too?"

"No," he said, shaking his head, "I'm going to be tied up here for a while. Tell everybody I said hello."

"I'll be glad to," she said.

*   *   *

The overcast sky had darkened since ten o'clock and a light rain was falling. A few people, some covering their heads with newspapers, stood in the street hailing taxis. The rain felt good to Deanie and she tipped her head back to catch the cool drops on her face.

She had had good luck catching a cab and now the driver was working his way uptown on the Avenue of the Americas. The slightly darkened streets and the rhythm of the windshield wipers, steady through the random pelting of wind-blown rain, invited remembrance and reflection, but each jolt and honk of the taxi brought her back to the present. Deanie watched the wipers going back and forth and back and forth and with a shock she saw the image of woman coming through the windshield. The rear-view mirror and its stem became her face and neck, and from her neck hung a long string of purple beads, a necklace swinging between two fan-shaped silvery breasts which were being worn away in layers with each sweep of the wiper blades. It was her mother. "Oh," she said, pulling her fists to her cheeks.

"You okay?" the cabby said.

Now she could see his large brown eyes in the rear-view mirror. She took a deep breath and nodded. "I'm okay."

"You sure?"

"Yes," she said, nodding, awed by how her mother's illness could show it's face.

* * *

The light turned green at 114th Street, and the cab made a U-turn around the island and stopped in front of the dark granite façade of the West End Cafe. Deanie paid the driver and hurried across the sidewalk.

Inside the old-time double-hinged doors she looked around the rectangular bar that nearly filled the front room and walked between the bar and the little cafeteria-style counter on her left towards the back room. There were about a dozen people at the bar, and a few sitting at the little tables along the wall on the right. The dark brown paneling of the barroom ended at the exposed bricks of the entrance to the back room and she saw Barett in a chair drawn up to the left end of one of the tables along the back wall. Next to him on the bench against the wall sat a black man she didn't recognize and Arnold Moskey. Kojo

71

sat in a chair at the other end of the table. They were all wearing shades, and they each had a drink. Eight or ten others were in the room—in the corner booth, at two of the center tables, and at tables along the wall to her right. Deanie went up the two steps to the back room and saw the black man wore a yellow and black garment that looked like a gown and had a brown and black kufi squarely on his head. He was resting his elbows on the table and gesturing with one hand as if he were sliding his words along an invisible surface that ran out from his chin. Arnold Moskey wore a short-sleeved white shirt, and Kojo was wearing a dark green knit shirt with three-quarter-length sleeves. Barett had rolled the sleeves of his tan shirt above his elbows. Kojo turned and seemed to look her way and Barett turned towards her and slid his sunglasses up to rest on top of his head.

"Hello," Barett said, "grab a chair." He pushed the empty chair back from the table and extended his arms towards her and the man who had been speaking. "Deanie Hollins, Henry Trainer."

The man nodded and smiled.

"Hello," she said.

"And you know Arnold Moskey, the good gray dean." Barett took a drink of his vodka and tonic. She smiled at Arnold Moskey and hung her bag on the back of her chair. Barett extended his arm towards Kojo. "And the Prince of Peeze."

"Is that so?" Kojo said.

"You are from a noble family," Barett said. "Aren't you?"

Kojo, not answering, sipped his drink and looked at her. "How are you, Deanie?"

"Fine." She flipped her hair back over her shoulders. So, he was from a noble family. Kojo had never mentioned that before. "I see you survived your party last night."

He lifted his eyebrows and leaned towards her. "Oh, yes," he said. "Not to worry."

"Something at the U. N.?" Arnold asked.

"Champagne and caviar," Barett said.

"That was last week," Kojo said. "Last night I went to a birthday party for a cousin in Newark."

"*Newark*," Barett said. "I thought you came to America to get *out* of the jungle."

"You have a cousin in Newark?" Arnold asked.

"Newark's full of our cousins," Henry said.

Kojo pointed at Henry. "That's right," he said. He pointed at Barett. "How about that?"

Barett laughed and took a drink.

"Tell me, Deanie," Kojo said, "did you actually ride all the way into the city with him?"

"Yes," she said. "But don't forget—Susan came along."

"I know," he said, laughing, "but it still must have been difficult."

Deanie shrugged. "It wasn't too bad," she said, smiling at Barett.

"Well," Kojo said, "let's hope he sleeps on the ride home."

"Are you going back on the train with us?"

"I'm afraid so," Kojo said. "Now what will you have to drink?"

"I think I'll have a glass of beer." As Deanie looked around for a waiter she realized that Henry Trainer was going on about something that he seemed really serious about. Arnold Moskey was listening, his hands clasped before him by a half-eaten sandwich. Barett was gesturing in a vaguely disruptive way. He had a mischievous look on his face, and his beard stood up in tufts where he had been pulling at it in his excitement.

"And we must concentrate on organization," Henry said. "We must channel the revolutionary ferment that is intensifying among black oppressed people. As the initiative is taken from the oppressor class by the acts of the people, we must drive the offensive forward to end oppression and exploitation."

"Drive the offensive forward," Barett said, clenching his fist on the table. "Right up the Hershey highway."

"We must consolidate our gains and defend them, and we must continue to do so as our struggle reaches higher levels of intensity."

"Higher levels of intensity," Barett said. He took a drink.

"The ruling racist cliques of the world must be broken up. The racist monster must be dismembered in whatever form it is found."

Barett shook an admonishing finger at her. "In whatever form."

"Our people in the cities are living in hellish conditions. The issues are of life and death. They must be mobilized now to confront the exploiter."

"Mobilize or walk, goddamnit," Barett shouted, shaking his fist in the air.

Kojo appeared to be deep in thought, perhaps weighing what Henry Trainer was saying, his head bent forward, his hands under the table. After a moment she realized that she was leaning towards him, and looking down in the direction of his apparent gaze, she saw that he was reading a newspaper on his lap.

Deanie leaned back in her chair, wondering what Kojo thought about Henry Trainer, and while he talked, the fact that she couldn't see Henry Trainer's eyes behind the dark glasses, and his lack of inflection made her feel that he was reading something written on the wall behind her, and for a instant she had an impulse to turn around and look—but she caught herself. Gradually Henry Trainer's speech settled into a drone and she heard only Barett's echoes and exclamations.

"Repressive apparatus. You bet," Barett said.

Deanie leaned over to Kojo. "Who is Henry Trainer?"

"He's one of Barett's old college chums. He teaches at City College and works in a bookstore."

"Why is Arnold Moskey here?"

"I think he happened to be in the bookstore when Barett went in to see Henry."

"Message of solidarity. Solid...grave importance...daily acts of aggression...political and economic destabilization."

"Right on, Henry." He pounded the table.

"Take it easy, Barett," Henry said, "you'll knock my drink over."

"Sorry." Barett took a drink, and Arnold Moskey took a bite of his sandwich.

"We must mount a massive assault on all fronts," Henry said. "We will never be crushed."

"Never be crushed," Barett said. He slid his fist out and knocked the ashtray off the table. "Whoops."

Henry stopped, and Barett lit a cigarette and picked up the ashtray. Barett had been having a good time with Henry, and she wondered why Kojo had shown so little interest in what Henry had been saying. Maybe Barett's interruptions had put him off. Or maybe he had been interested. Or maybe it was something else. She had promised herself that she'd try to live in uncertainties without getting messed up, but she was beginning to feel that she was wondering herself into a mass of mental quicksand. She would step back. "When do you expect Susan?" she asked Barett.

He sighed and checked his watch. "She was supposed to be at her career until one-thirty. She should be here pretty soon. Though if she sees Henry wearing a dress she might not want to stay."

Henry frowned, looked towards Arnold and Kojo, and then from behind his shades he seemed to be looking at her. "Your consciousness needs to be raised, Barett. I think you should do a little homework." He smiled, showing two gold teeth.

"I have been. And you know what I've concluded?"

Henry ran his hand over his mustache, stroked his neatly-trimmed goatee, and looked towards Arnold. "What have you concluded, Barett?"

Barett tapped his cigarette on the ashtray. "I've concluded that Marxism isn't thriving because it couldn't show how two or more people—mother and child especially—should reap the rewards of the same bowel movement."

"Money as excrement," Arnold said.

"There's nothing new about that theory," Henry said.

"No," Barett said, "that's not what I'm saying. The mother says, '*We* labored to produce that product, that turd.' The capitalist takes the turd for his own use, and even pays wages for it—but not enough wages." He took a drink. "Because the capitalist has forgotten who all"—he tapped the table to emphasize "all"—"who all produced it. He ignores the mother."

"'Heaven has no rage like love to hatred turned,'" Arnold Moskey quoted.

"'Nor hell a fury like a woman scorned,'" Barett said. "As a matter of fact, Marx was like a mother with a tremendous chip on her shoulder—trying to write about universal potty training."

"Is that a buffalo chip?" Henry asked.

The comment seemed to throw Barett off track. "A buffalo chip?"

"That's a turd. I thought maybe you were going to include animals in your—" He hesitated and stirred the air with his hand. "Your conclusion."

Barett's eyes widened in delight and he put his arm around Henry's shoulders. "That's marvelous, Henry."

Kojo's shoulders rose and fell a few times as if he was laughing to himself. But she couldn't tell if he was laughing with them or at them.

"So," Deanie asked, "you're saying that capitalists don't give enough credit to the producer of the producer—and so on?"

"Right," Barett said. "You get an 'A' for that."

She smiled at his comment—and then she felt a twinge of annoyance at having been given a grade. She had been part of the group at the table, and then Barett had, in a way, redefined her as a student. They were professors, and right in the middle of everything Barett had reestablished an invisible partition that she felt had given her a different status at the table. "So you're talking about a long stream of shit?" she said.

"Well—"

"He's *talking* a long stream of shit," Henry interrupted.

"That's inevitable," Kojo said. She couldn't tell whether he was agreeing with Henry or commenting on something else.

"Now wait a minute," Barett said, "just wait a minute."

"There's nothing more inevitable than a bowel movement," Arnold Moskey said, laying his shades on the table. He rubbed the bridge of his nose, and they seemed to be waiting for him to say something else. She watched his thick eyebrows rise and fall above his fingers. He put his shades back on and rested his clasped hands on the table. She noticed the extinguished cigarette butt dangling from the corner of his lip. Over it his gray mustache was tar-stained from smoke.

"You can slow it down," Barett went on, "or you can speed it up, but you can't stop a bowel movement."

"I have to make a phone call," Kojo said, getting up from the table. "Deanie, order me a coffee, please."

*   *   *

Kojo was twirling his cup in a small circle on the table, watching the coffee swirl around inside.

"Okay, Henry," Barett said, "art reflects social conditions. But what about the kind of work that for the most part is about the artist's longing and search for joy? I mean"—he paused and pulled at his beard—"goddamnit, what about masturbation fantasies? You still haven't said where they fit."

"Bend over and I'll show you where they fit," Henry said.

"No way." He laughed and leaned toward Deanie as if to keep Henry from hearing him. "I should have warned you," he said, looking from her to Kojo to Arnold, "it's not safe to bend over in the same room with Henry."

Henry sighed and shook his head. "What am I going to do with you, Barry?"

"Barry?" he said, wide-eyed, and laughing. "Whoa! I know what you're *not* gonna do."

77

Their waiter came up to the table and looked at Barett. "Barett Burkhart?"

"Yes."

"Your wife's on the phone." He pointed towards the phone and picked up Arnold's sandwich plate. "Everybody okay?"

"Some more coffee, please," Kojo said. "Deanie?"

"I'm fine, thanks." She still had half a glass of beer.

"We're leaving soon," Arnold said, gesturing towards Henry.

The waiter picked up Barett's drink, wiped under it, and set it back on the thick wooden table.

As Barett came back to the table Arnold slid out some dollar bills and some change for a tip.

"The career woman's running late," Barett said. "I'm going to meet her at a restaurant in Rockefeller Center." He sat down and took a swallow of his vodka and tonic. "Do you want to come along?" He looked at her, and gestured towards Kojo.

"Not today," Kojo said. "I don't feel like going all the way to Rockefeller Center."

Deanie felt the same way. "I'll meet you at Penn Station," she said.

"We'll both meet you at Penn Station," Kojo said. "What would be a good time, Deanie?"

"Five?"

"Sounds all right," Barett said. "That'll give me time to check out a couple of bookstores."

Arnold was chuckling as Henry got up to go, and he stood up with his paper napkin still tucked in his pants.

"We've got to run," Henry said.

"You've got the runs?" Barett asked.

Henry sighed. He extended his hand palm-up to Deanie and gently clasped her fingers. "Nice meeting you." He gave vigorous, fraternal, tipped-up hand grips to Kojo and Barett. "Keep the faith," he said.

Arnold Moskey looked around the table. "Safe traveling." He leaned across to Barett. "Stick to your romantic guns."

"It's a big one," Barett said.

As Arnold Moskey and Henry Trainer went down the steps into the front room, napkin and all, and became silhouettes going around the bar, Barett finished his drink and slid back his chair. "I'm going to meet Susan now. We'll see you at the Port Jeff gate at five."

Deanie nodded and Kojo lifted his hand in a salute. "Five." He took a drink of coffee and leaned back in his chair as Barett headed for the door.

"What did he mean by 'romantic guns?'" Deanie asked.

"Knowing Arnold, I'd say that he was probably referring to Barett's excitement about self-expression, his fanciful way of seeing things sometimes. Barett"—he paused, gesturing with his hand as if to find a word—"Barett even heard 'gun'—though that's not what Arnold said."

"That's right," she said. "He *did* say 'guns.' But maybe Barett heard 'guns' and twisted it to 'gun.'"

"Maybe so." He raised his eyebrows.

"Wouldn't that be a kind of linguistic imperialism?" she said.

Kojo laughed. "Linguistic imperialism?" He laughed again and stroked his goatee.

"And also—when he responded to Henry by asking him if he had the runs?" Deanie said.

"That's good, Deanie," Kojo said. "Barett Burkhart, the linguistic imperialist." His eyebrows went way up, and laughing, he tipped back his chair. "We'll have to bug Barett about that." He finished his coffee. "So much for romantic guns."

She took a drink. "But they did mention guns earlier, when you went to the phone, and I didn't know if romantic guns was supposed to mean something else."

"Well, I must say that if you gave Barett—I don't know about Henry—," he paused, "—Arnold did in fact train to fight against Franco—," he paused again, "—if you gave Barett a gun it would be very definitely a romantic gun. He's never been shot at."

"Have you?"

"A time or two."

They both fell silent. Kojo suddenly seemed more interesting to her. She knew it didn't take brains to get shot at, but from what she knew of him, she imagined that he had been engaged in something out of the ordinary. She wondered what the circumstances had been. Deanie finished her beer, smiled, and shrugged. "I was just wondering," she said.

"Not to worry," he said. He pushed his coffee cup away and adjusted his shades. "You said they were talking about guns," Kojo said. "What were they saying?"

"They were talking about the protests here and wondering what ever happened to some of the people who were involved."

"Protests? Here?"

"Just a while back at the end of the 60's at Columbia—just a couple of blocks away." Kojo was looking at her, apparently waiting for her to continue. "They started out as protests against the university's plans to build a gymnasium in Morningside Park, which would have deprived the locals, mostly black people, of recreational space." Kojo brought his elbows up to the table and rested his chin on his clasped hands. "Then the protesters took over some campus buildings and the SDS got involved."

"Society of Demonstrating Students?"

"That's probably what the trustees thought—only it was Students for a Democratic Society."

"Oh, yes," he said, nodding and rubbing his goatee across his knuckles, "I've read about them." He paused. "Tell me," he went on, "how do you know about these things?"

"Well, for one thing, one of the teaching assistants in one of my classes said she was involved in them when she was a student at Columbia. And she talked about them a lot."

"I see. And what became of the issue of the threatened recreational space?"

Deanie felt pressure growing in her neck and ears. She didn't know, and she thought she should know. She thought Kojo expected her to know. She sighed and clicked her thumbnail on her tooth. "I'm sorry, I don't know."

"Oh!" he said. "A serious lack of follow-through." She felt a little annoyed with herself and must have looked it. He smiled. "Not to worry." He laughed. "You've been busy with school, and, indeed, so have I. I haven't been able to keep track of a lot of things out there." He swept his arm in a semicircle. His comments had a calming effect and she relaxed.

"I'm glad to hear that," she said. He smiled. "So what are you working on?"

"Oral traditions, folklore, but, to get back to what we were saying, did Barett make any imaginative claims for me in his talk about guns?"

"No." She smiled and flipped her hair back over her shoulders. "He didn't mention you at all."

"I'm glad," Kojo said. "Barett has a very busy imagination sometimes."

Deanie nodded. "Sometimes."

"Let's have a sandwich," he said.

"Why don't we go someplace else for a sandwich?" she said. "I don't want to sit here all day."

"Good idea," he said.

"Then you can tell me how you got shot at."

"If you insist."

It had stopped raining. Outside on Broadway Kojo glanced in each direction, and Deanie, with her hands sunk in the rear pockets of her jeans, tipped her head to indicate they should head up the street towards Columbia. Kojo stepped around to her side, and after a few brisk steps in the damp heat they slowed to a stroll.

"Let's see," Kojo said. "I'd better fill you in a bit on my background. I can't have Barett's exaggerations—whenever they may come up—bandied about as history."

"Or brandied about as history."

"Aha!" He laughed. "That's good, Deanie. 'Brandied about as history.'" He laughed again. "I'll have to remember that."

They went across Broadway and 114th Street to the edge of the campus and continued up to 116th Street, where they cut over towards Morningside Drive.

"Hamilton Hall is in that direction," Deanie said, pointing to her left. "That's the building the black students took over." A couple who had been lingering by a doorway meandered away through the heat. "You were going to tell me about getting shot at."

"Well, all right. Let's keep walking around the block," he said, pointing ahead and adjusting his shades. "Your city is New York, and when I was your age, my city was Keta. When I was still at home it took us a couple of hours by wagon to reach the city and over an hour to reach the ocean.

"The district secondary school was walking distance from our village, so I missed very little school. I enjoyed school, but what I really enjoyed was swimming.

"One of our favorite pastimes was called 'the dive for life.' We used it as a measure of courage and as a test to determine who could go swimming with us when we went to the ocean. What we did was to dive about thirty feet from the edge of a rocky cliff that ringed a deep cove. We only dove at safe tide, but we had to swim down about twenty feet and squeeze through a hole in the rock that was so narrow that you had to put one arm through and then pull and kick your way through until your shoulders were through. Then you could pull your other arm through. But that's not all. There was a down and up bend in the hole, and in order to get through it—the hole was perhaps three feet through"—he held his hands out, looking from one to the other—"you had to roll over and go through on your back. You had to go down in order to go up." He made a diving and return gesture with his hand. "And if you made it you got to keep coming."

"And if you didn't make it?"

"You could try again."

"Could you cheat?"

"No. Someone would always dive with you until you made it through once."

"Did anybody ever get in trouble?"

"One fellow did drown—but he was full of palm wine and he had grown fat. It took two of us three dives to pull him out. But he was still dead."

He paused and looked as if he was watching some huge threatening thing moving slowly up Morningside Drive into Harlem. Deanie looked, but couldn't tell what, if anything, he was watching.

"Sometimes we would time the diving to see who could do it the fastest. I did win a few times and it got so that—so it seemed—I could have made the dive in my sleep. But it wasn't easy."

"I'll buy that."

"You'll buy what?"

"I mean that I agree with you. It sounds really hard."

"Oh. I thought perhaps you wanted to buy the dive for life story." He shook his head and looked as if he couldn't believe what he was thinking. "Seriously, once a folklorist from the University of Indiana came to our school, our secondary school, saying that he would pay us for every tradition we could relate to him. So my friends got together and cooked up at least thirty"—he paused and held up his hands as if to frame what he was about to say—"traditions"—he paused again and shook his head, "for him, and he tape-recorded them all and took them back to Indiana."

"Did he publish them?"

"I never heard. I hope he didn't. Unless he was being considered for tenure—he may have. He would have been publishing brandied history." He looked towards Morningside Drive again. "And we don't need that sort of thing." Kojo paused. "I used to do a lot of wood carving"—his tone was lower, his words came slower—"small figures and designs—but then in secondary school the carved wood that I found most

83

often in my hands was the stock of a gun—actually a Lee-Enfield carbine. We used to drill with three carbines and a number of sticks cut to the length of the guns. On rare occasions we had live ammunition for target practice." Kojo stopped talking, took off his shades, and stretched his arms out.

"What's a carbine?" she said.

"A short-barreled rifle."

"So how were you shot at?"

He put his shades back on, ran his hand over his head, and brought it to rest on his neck. "There came a time when I was called upon to defend our village from several attackers. We didn't know who they represented or what forces they had marshaled. As it turned out, it was a marriage dispute, and it was over in fifteen minutes. But it was real. Lives were lost."

"You were in secondary school?"

"Yes." They kept walking. She felt better walking. The rhythm of the walking seemed to temper his talk of lives being lost. "And," Kojo went on, "there was an incident in the borderland with bullets flying around. After that I returned to London where I met Susan."

Deanie figured that "incident" meant that Kojo didn't want to go into details. "Shall we get a sandwich now?"

"Why not?"

They walked to the corner and turned down Broadway. After a while she pointed to a deli a few doors away. "Over there?"

"Fine." They crossed the street, went past a brick church, and crossed another street.

"So," she went on, "when did you return to London?"

"Let me see. I went back to London in the autumn five or six years ago. I had taken my degree there, so I still had quite a few acquaintances around—some of whom worked for the BBC and had connections for film projects. So I made out all right until I met Susan Anderson."

"Until?"

"I mean I was doing well away from home and then I met Susan, and now here I am."

Deanie gave him a sidelong look and her version of a playful smile that said she wasn't quite satisfied with his answer. What he had just said seemed a little rushed, forced almost, and she wanted him to know that she had noticed.

His eyes caught hers for a split second, and he turned to the menu taped on the deli window. "After you," he said.

She flipped her hair back over her shoulders and they went in past the cashier's stand. The air-conditioning was a relief and the smells of hot pastrami and sausage and peppers made her mouth water. Two women with a little girl five or six years old were on line ahead of them, and a frizzy-haired young woman with a canvas book bag over her shoulder was paying for a cup of soup. Deanie stood looking over the food, rubbing her finger on the glass showcase along the counter. Kojo was bent over next to her looking at the trays of food. The white-haired counterman stood opposite her, his cheeks glowing pink in the bright fluorescent light. His fingers tapped the blade of a butcher knife that he held flat on the cutting board. The two women and the child moved to the cash register.

"Miss?" the counterman said, waiting for Deanie to order.

"Just a second," Deanie said. "It all looks so good."

"What'll you have, dude?"

When Deanie heard that she momentarily shut her eyes and felt her pulse run up till it throbbed in her temples.

"Dude?" Kojo said. "Dude?" He turned away and bent and leaned as if he was looking around for someone. "I don't seem to see a dude. Or do you mean the cashier?"

The cashier was about twenty-five. He was pale, pimply, and looked like he hadn't slept for a week. He wore a tall chef's hat that leaned way out and made him look like he was going to fall over. He was giving change to one of the women. The frizzy-haired woman went out.

The counterman didn't answer.

"Let's go," Deanie said.

The two women and the child went out.

"We must find the dude," Kojo said. "Unless he's the cashier."

Deanie watched the counterman scratch his cheek and look towards the cashier. He looked like he was beginning to sense that he had his hands full.

"Hey, Jimmy," the counterman shouted, "you want a sandwich?"

The cashier looked startled. "What?"

"Do you want a sandwich?"

"Do I want a sandwich?"

"Yeah, dude, a sandwich."

The cashier stared at the three of them. "Sure."

"You'll have to wait."

The cashier shrugged and began sorting a handful of receipts.

"Now what can I do for you, Miss?"

"Nothing, thank you." Deanie moved towards the door.

"Anything for you?" the counterman said, looking over Kojo's head.

"Do you have sliced crocodile?"

"Oh, Jesus, Joseph, and Mary," the counterman said, looking down at the cutting board.

"Well?" Kojo said.

The counterman started brushing scraps of lettuce off the counter into his hand.

"Well, do you?" Kojo asked.

"No," he said, still brushing scraps into his hand.

"Do you think I could get some?"

The man shrugged and sighed.

"Let's go," Deanie said.

Kojo looked at her and nodded. "We have to go," Kojo said, leaning towards the counterman. "And if I ever want sliced crocodile, I'm going to come here first." Kojo leaned back from the counter. "Well, my friend," he said to her, "let's go."

The counterman started moving away, wiping his hands on his apron.

After they'd gone about twenty yards up the street Deanie turned to Kojo. "You know something, Kojo?"

"You're still hungry?"

"Yes, but there's something else."

"What?"

"That's the first time anybody older than I has ever actually called me a friend."

"Well, it's about time," he said.

FIVE

After they changed trains in Jamaica Deanie dozed fitfully by the window as they rocked and clanked through Queens on the way out to Port Jefferson Station. Fitfully, she saw the tops of trees, a woman in a fourth-floor window working a clothesline pulley, a clanging crossing signal, more trees. Susan sat across from her, reading a paperback. Barett had left Susan's side to go to the bar car for cigarettes. Kojo, still wearing his sunglasses, sat next to Deanie, reading a magazine. She had just heard the conductor announce Smithtown. She remembered a lot of people getting off in Hicksville. She didn't remember hearing any of the other stops announced. She would keep her eyes closed, and maybe she could go back to sleep for the few minutes left. "You've got to give it to me. You've got to give it to me," the wheels were saying to the tracks. "You've got to give it to me. You've got to give it to me." Okay, Zerk, give it to me, give it to me, give it to me, give it to me. *When I called you this morning I couldn't say what I wanted to say. How could you not have known that? You were always such a great listener, everybody saying how you really heard and really understood. Why couldn't you hear me saying I love you over and over again? You didn't want to admit it. Your old girlfriend—what did she say? Why was she there? To see if there was still anything going on? Then this noon when I called my words had nothing in them, nothing between the lines. I'm glad you weren't there. Or maybe you were there and didn't answer. I'm almost empty and I need you more than ever, but I can't keep going on like this. If you want to keep going in some other direction I've got to let you keep going and close the door behind you and when I'm totally empty I won't need you because there won't be anything that needs anything and then I can get along without you and I won't ever care if you're never ever there. You may not believe it, but I could do it. Could you believe me? Maybe you didn't always. Or maybe you didn't believe in me. Maybe that's it. Maybe you never believed in me. I guess you didn't have to believe in me to come in me. You used to really care for your friend. Did you love her? I could tell on the phone something was different, something was missing. I guess I was missing. I don't care. Please be there when I get back.*

*   *   *

"You've got to give it to me. You've got to give it to me," the wheels were saying to the tracks. "You've got to give it to me. You've got to give it to me." No, that's not the train. It must be somebody's radio. Just a few more minutes of sleep. Her eyes barely opened. Kojo was sitting next to Susan, his hand resting on hers. "You've got to give it to me," he said. "Your desire for partnership, or whatever you want to call it, will surely lead to destruction."

"No, it won't," Susan said.

89

"It will." He must have seen her eyelids move. He lifted his hand from Susan's and adjusted his sunglasses. "Deanie's waking up," he said.

"Did you rest well?" Susan asked.

"I got a few winks."

"Kojo wants my book." She fanned through the pages both ways with her thumbs like a gambler shuffling cards. "Should I give it to him?"

Kojo's remark about partnership and destruction was fascinating, and she could tell the paperback wasn't what he wanted. She could also see they wanted to take her past whatever they had been talking about. She would go along with them.

"Are you finished with it?" she said.

"Well," Susan, said, "I thought I was."

"If you're not sure," Deanie said, "keep it."

Kojo raised his eyebrows and looked at Susan.

She smiled, fanned the pages three more times, and dropped the book into her bag. "I think I'll keep it," she said.

Kojo rolled up his magazine and slowly tapped it in the palm of his hand. The raised eyebrows, the finger resting on the goatee, the looks of playful inquisitiveness from the afternoon had vanished from his face. He looked dead serious. Susan was looking out the window. He looked dead serious about getting something from Susan. The way they sat there, looking in opposite directions, made Deanie feel uncomfortable. She wished she knew what it was that he wanted. She felt a chill. She'd find out what he wanted, she told herself, but this wasn't the time to ask.

* * *

About halfway to the Peeze campus from the train station, Barett wheeled Susan's car into a gas station. He looked through his wallet and turned to Susan. "Got a credit card?"

"Don't you have any money?"

"Some—but I might have to go out to get some milk for Gary."

"Milk for the *baby*," Susan said. "Give me a break."

The attendant, a fellow in his twenties with long stringy hair, came up to the window. "Fill it?"

Susan found the credit card and handed it to Barett.

"Sure," Barett said.

The attendant hesitated and peered into the car before turning to the gas pump. Deanie glanced at Kojo. He had taken his shades off and was looking at his magazine. The attendant stuck the nozzle into the filler pipe, and walked back to the four guys and the girl hanging out by the garage door. They were all wearing jeans and stencilled T-shirts. Three of the guys looked to be about Deanie's age. The girl and one fellow looked a little older. They all were looking towards the car and seemed to be discussing something about it. After a minute they all walked up to the front of the car, and the attendant came back to Deanie's door, where he bent over to rinse a squeegee in a bucket. The others hadn't moved.

"What are they looking at?" Susan asked.

"I don't know," Barett said, "maybe there're some body parts stuck on your bumper." Susan turned back to Deanie and rolled her eyes. Kojo looked up and smiled for the first time since they'd left the train. The attendant handed the squeegee to the young woman, and she started cleaning the windshield on Susan's side. Barett yawned. "Probably on-the-job training," he said, yawning again.

The attendant walked back and replaced the nozzle.

"Am I right?" the attendant called out.

"What?" Barett asked. The attendant was looking towards the young woman with the squeegee.

"Yes!" she screamed. "He's the one! The guy with the fly balls!"

"What are they talking about?" Susan asked.

"I don't have the slightest idea," Barett said. He started the car and inadvertently turned the key again, grinding the starter.

91

They were all laughing and gesturing with their hands.

"The guy with the fly balls!" someone shouted again.

"What are they talking about?" Susan asked.

"I don't know," Barett said, "and I'm not going to wait around to find out." He put the car in gear.

"What's going on?" Kojo whispered to Deanie.

She shook her head. "I'll tell you later," she whispered.

"How do you play closet baseball?" someone yelled.

"With a little tiny bat," came the answer. Everyone outside roared.

Barett stomped the accelerator, throwing them back in their seats in a screech of tires. He hit the brakes and threw them forward as he screeched up to the street.

"Stop it!" Susan screamed. "You'll kill us all!"

Barett leaned over the steering wheel. "Just as soon as this truck gets past—"

"Don't," Susan said. "You left my credit card." Barett's head dropped to rest on the steering wheel. "Are you going to get it—or shall I?" she said.

His shoulders rose and fell in a deep sigh. He backed the car away from the street, got out, and walked back to where the attendant was standing with the card and the receipt to be signed. The guys and the girl had all mercifully gone back by the garage where they stood quietly with their hands in their pockets. Or maybe they saw how big Barett was when he stood up, and they weren't going to take any chances.

"Was that about Iris's party?" Susan asked, turning towards Deanie. She gestured to indicate that Susan was putting her in an uncomfortable position. "Never mind. It must have been. I heard about a couple of people getting caught in a closet. The guy must have been Barett." Susan ran her fingers through her hair, and when Barett reached for the door she sighed and turned back to look out her window. "He'll risk anything for a blow job," she said. Deanie glanced at Kojo. His shades were on and he seemed to be looking at his hands, folded in his lap. He looked like he could have been meditating, or perhaps he was trying to sleep.

As Barett drove past the brightly lit gas station sign Deanie saw Susan's cheeks trembling ever so slightly, her eyelids fluttering, and though she couldn't see any tears, she knew, as the car headed into the countryside, that she must have been crying.

* * *

As they drove up to Kojo's apartment, Deanie was thrilled to see Zerk and a couple of guys on the court shooting baskets.

"Thanks for the ride," Kojo said.

"Good night," Susan said.

"I'll get out here too," Deanie said.

Barett lit a cigarette. "So long, Deanie."

"I'll get a ride with Zerk," she said.

The campus was refreshingly quiet in the early evening. The cool tones of the blue spruce, the dark green rhododendron, and the blue hydrangea seemed to ripple along the bricks around Kojo's patio as Deanie and Kojo approached his apartment door.

"It sounds like Barett is in trouble," Kojo laughed.

"I think so," she said. "He got caught with his pants down, literally, in a closet with a friend of mine at that party that night you stopped by on your way to the city."

He nodded. "The party I missed," he said, laughing a little.

It seemed like a good time to ask about the friction, or whatever it was, with Susan on the train. "Can you tell me what you and Susan were discussing when I was waking up?"

"Waking up?" he said.

"On the train," she said.

"Well," he said, pausing. He smiled as he glanced at her. "I'll tell you soon enough. This just isn't the time."

"You seem to be under a lot of pressure."

"Do you think so?"

"Yes, I do," she said. "You ought to take a break and do something relaxing for a while."

"Ah," he said, "you strike a chord there. I really miss fishing." He threw his arm out and pointed. "And the Long Island Sound is so close."

She nodded. "Then you should go fishing."

"You're right," he said. He paused. "Well, I'm going in now. I have to call some friends in the city who want to come out to visit."

"Maybe you could take them fishing," she said.

"Not a bad idea," he said, reaching for his door.

"Bye," she said. She walked towards the court. She could tell that Zerk had been watching her. He was resting his foot on the basketball and wiping the sweat from his face with his red T-shirt. His buddies were sitting on the grass, taking a break. He smiled and started towards her.

"Have a good time?" he asked.

"Yes," she said, nodding. She just didn't feel like saying anything about what had happened at the gas station. "Are you ready to go?"

"Sure," he said. He kicked the ball back towards his buddies and waved goodby to them.

*   *   *

They left Zerk's car by his place and now they were walking and carrying their shoes along the drive towards the gatehouse. The pinks and silvers of the sunset were beginning to fill the sky, and the cool grass felt good under her feet.

"So how's the job going?" he said.

"Okay. I got over fifteen hours in last week."

"That's what I figured," he said.

"I made over two hundred dollars and only missed one class."

"All right," he said enthusiastically, "if you did that forty hours a week you could charter your own plane in September."

"Maybe not to Naples."

"Naples, Florida, maybe," he said.

"Maybe."

"Or Venice, Florida."

"Or maybe Rome, New York," she paused and threw her arms out, "or Palermo, Oklahoma."

"Well..." his voice trailed off. "Ever been to Palermo, Oklahoma?"

"No."

"Good."

"Why?" she asked.

"There isn't such a place."

"How do you know?"

"I was stationed at Ft. Sill for a while, and spent some time reading maps in case I had to get out of Oklahoma in a hurry."

"Huh," she sighed.

"What?"

"What do they know?"

"Well..."

"What if I really, really desired to go there?"

He shrugged.

Deanie wondered what he'd say next, but he didn't say anything at all, and they kept walking towards the gatehouse. She remembered seeing his former girlfriend's car and all of the feelings that it had aroused, but now all of that seemed a really long time ago, and without any effort at all she let go of the remembrance and it faded away. She saw some red petunias at the end of her parking area, and she stopped to look at them, brushing her toes across the soft green leaves, thinking that if she really desired to go to Palermo, Oklahoma, she would go.

As they came up to her porch she felt better than she'd felt all day, and she sat on the top step, and when Zerk sat next to her she rested her head on his shoulder and ran her hand along his arm and over to his damp chest where she made little circles in the hair. Now she could feel his hand gently along her side and over her breast and up to her chin where he lifted her face to meet his kiss.

"You're going to stay with me tonight?" he said. "Okay?"

She nodded, sliding her hand along his thigh. "As long as what's-her-name isn't there," she said.

"Come on," he said. "We had something to eat and then she drove out to Riverhead to try to sell a company some copy machines."

"If you say so," she said, digging her fingers into his thigh.

SIX

"Waiting for somebody?"

Deanie yawned as if the question had increased her need for oxygen.

"Some friends," she answered.

The old man held his eyes on her a moment, squinting in the late morning sun, and then returned to stacking a dozen or so lobster pots on the edge of the dock. Farther down sea gulls fluttered back and forth from the deck to the piling that stuck up along the edge every twelve or fifteen feet.

Deanie was sitting on a wooden pile, tapping her sneakers on one of the old tires hung below the edge to cushion the dock and the boats that tied up there. Till the old man spoke Deanie had forgotten about going blue fishing on the sound.

Earlier in the week she had told Susan about Kojo's wanting to go fishing, and in no time at all Susan had gotten some boating information from the Mt. Sinai Marina, which was not far from Peeze Point, and she had called Randall in the city, and then she had gotten a promise from Kojo that he'd be there with his friends who were coming out to visit.

Till the old man spoke Deanie had forgotten about the whole thing. As soon as she had slid out of the back seat of Susan's car she walked across the marina, her gaze lost in the blue of sky and water. And while Susan and Barett were inside the office putting down a deposit on a boat big enough to hold half a dozen people she sat there taking in the scenery.

Deanie looked towards the marina office. Susan and Barett were still inside. A couple of sea gulls crying to the wind floated overhead and dropped to land on an old church pew placed on the dock for sightseers. Deanie slid off the pile, watched the gulls fly off, and with her thumbs hooked in her jeans walked to the pew and sat gazing into the distance. A white sail bobbed on the horizon and the blue of sky and water seemed to radiate from it in all directions. It all looked like a huge stained glass window against the sky, and she felt drawn to it, as if with the right word or combination of words she could soar to it and pass through to the other side and just keep going. Once again she remembered the Otis Redding song and was sittin' on the dock of the bay, watching the tide roll away...and she smelled smoke.

Susan was standing by her with a cigarillo and Barett was walking up folding a yellow piece of paper that looked like a receipt.

"Is everything all set?" Deanie asked.

"We're all set," Barett said. "Randall might be a little let down, but I'm not going to worry about it."

"What do you mean?"

"We thought we could rent a big boat so Randall could play the captain," Susan said. "But they just rent small boats, so we had to charter the one we wanted, and the captain comes with it." She pointed to a clean white cabin cruiser tied up about twenty yards past where the old man had been stacking lobster pots. "It's a 1961 Wheeler. Does that mean anything to you?"

"Wheeler-dealer, side-wheeler," she said, pausing, "wheel be over for dinner..." She threw up her hands and shrugged.

"She's solid," Barett said, "all wood. They're the best, none of that fiberglass stuff." He sighed and dug into his shirt pocket for a cigarette. "Sixty-one was a good year for Wheeler."

With Barett's authoritative sounding comment the conversation faded, and they watched a short stocky man wearing a black T-shirt, aviator sunglasses, and a red baseball cap carry a bag of gear from a shed by the office to the cabin cruiser, her chrome sparkling in the sun.

"Must be the captain," Barett said.

"Is she very expensive?" Deanie asked, thinking it might be fun to sail to Block Island or Nantucket sometime.

"Not for a forty-eight footer with twin diesels," Barett said. "In any case, Randall's paying half, and we figured two or three hours out would be long enough. Then we can go to Kojo's place for a drink and maybe shoot a few baskets." He raised his hands over his head, rose up on his toes, and shot some crumpled cellophane from a cigarette package towards the water, but the breeze caught it, and it looped up to fall back on the deck beside him.

"Litterbug," Susan said.

"At least my litter doesn't hurt anything," Barett said as he picked up the cellophane, "or anybody."

Susan looked at Deanie and sighed. "I came here for a good time," she said.

"So did I," Barett said, looking at Deanie.

"Me too," she said, and she stood up, stretched her arms in the breeze, took a deep breath, and watched the man return to the shed and carry a cooler and a case of beer back to the boat.

"He's the captain all right," Barett said.

"How can you tell?" Deanie asked.

"He's got the beer and the cooler."

The mild breeze blew Susan's hair across her face and she held her cigarillo before her eye as if it were a tiny telescope pointed towards the horizon. When she wanted to smoke she swept the hair from her lips with the thumb of her other hand. The breeze stirred the slight curls of Barett's hair to rise and fall like random bursts of cooking popcorn. He was also staring towards the horizon, though, Deanie noticed, he was looking east towards London and Susan was looking north towards New London. Susan's thumb was hooked over the top of her embroidered jeans and Barett's left hand hung loosely in the pocket of his baggy pants. Deanie saw how the bottoms of his pant legs were frayed where his heels had caught them, and she wondered what he had meant about his litter not hurting anybody, and whether he was trying to say something about Susan, and she wondered whether Susan had found out about whatever was going on between Barett and Iris.

"What time did you tell everyone to be here?" Barett asked.

"Around eleven-thirty," Susan said. She checked her watch. "Won't be long."

"I'm going to get some cigarettes," he said. "Want anything?"

"No thanks," Susan said.

He looked at Deanie, raised his eyebrows quizzically, and bit at the edge of his mustache.

"I'll go along," Deanie said.

Inside the office Barett emptied his pocket on the glass counter top to find change for the cigarette machine. Along with the change were some loose keys, a book of matches from the Shamrock Tavern, and the crumpled cellophane. Deanie picked up the cellophane and looked around for a wastebasket. Across the counter was a desk where a white-haired woman sat leafing through a phone book. Behind her on a long oak table was a shortwave radio that occasionally blurted static and undecipherable phrases from the marine traffic on the sound. The pale green walls were covered with antique-looking dark-framed pictures of sailing ships and out-of-date pinup calendars advertising lubricants and filters for marine engines. She saw the wastebasket on the other side of Barett by the cigarette machine and threw the cellophane straight into it.

"Two points," she said.

"Nice shot," Barett said. "You can be on my team."

"Thanks," Deanie said. "I'll think about it." And then she told herself, yes, I'll really have to think about it.

Barett gave a thumbs-up sign and took his cigarettes from the machine.

*   *   *

Randall's limousine was pulled up next to Susan's car at the edge of the gravel parking lot. Out on the deck of the marina Randall and Susan stood talking. Occasionally Susan swept her arm across the horizon, looking as if she was trying to sell Randall some real estate on the opposite shore. Smells of drying seaweed and fish bait breezed by in a light gust of wind. As Deanie and Barett walked across the planks in the glaring sun she looked down and recalled a saying she used to hear on her way to school, "Step on a crack and you'll break your mother's back." She picked up her feet and tiptoed from plank to plank and before long she was imagining that she was striking the bars of a giant marimba that stretched out to sea.

"You okay?" Barett asked. He looked puzzled.

"Yes," she said. "The deck reminded me of a marimba and I was looking for a tune."

"I see," he said, puffing his cigarette. "For a couple of seconds you looked a little off balance."

"Not to worry."

"That's what Kojo says."

"Not to worry," she repeated. "I wonder where he is."

"Not to worry," he said.

She laughed.

"Randall," Barett said, greeting his brother.

"Howdy," he said.

Deanie nodded. "Hello."

"How was the ride out?" Barett asked.

"Okay," he said. "A few potholes on the expressway, but they'd been filled up with little sports cars and motorcycles, so I just went right over 'em." He swept his hand around palm-down to indicate how smooth the ride had been.

"So you drove out?" Deanie asked.

"For a change," he said.

Deanie thought she heard something thumping, like somebody knocking on a door, and Susan frowned as if she had heard it too.

"What?" Randall said.

Deanie heard the thumping again—coming from the planks under their feet.

"Is that you, Marimba Foot?" Barett asked.

"No," she said, shrugging, "I thought it was your heart palpitating."

Barett rolled his eyes, tapped the ashes off his cigarette, and pointed it at Randall.

"Maybe the sea gulls are getting Randall aroused," he said. "Maybe there's something thumping in his jeans."

Deanie didn't pay any attention to Barett's remark to his brother. It was part of a routine that sometimes surfaced when they were together. She was peering down, trying to see down between the planks to see what had caused the noise.

"Step aside, Needle-Dick," Randall said. He bent over next to Deanie and peered down, shielding his eyes with his hands.

"At least I can keep it up," Barett said.

"It's dark down there," Susan said, "I can't see a thing."

"Susan!" The shout came from below the deck.

"What is it?" Susan shouted.

"Oh, do not ask, 'What is it?' Let us go and—watch out!—"

Deanie heard a yell and a splash—like someone falling overboard—and several voices garbled together in a watery commotion.

"Kojo?" Susan shouted, going to the edge of the marina. "Is that you?" Barett followed her and they got down on their hands and knees and leaned out to look underneath.

"Is that Kojo down there?" Randall asked.

"I don't know," Deanie said as she got down next to Susan, "let's see." Randall got down beside her and they both leaned over the edge.

Coming towards them into the light was Kojo, facing them, seated in the front of a gray skiff, holding his hand to his brow in a formal gesture of salute. Behind him someone moved the oars and behind the oarsmen were two other figures.

"Lef-tenant Kojo Dedu reporting for duty, Suh!" he announced, apparently to none of them in particular. He threw the salute and the boat slid out into the brighter light and turned parallel to the marina. Kojo sat straight, resting his hands on his knees. He was wearing jeans and an old army shirt. The oarsman and one of the others wore dark cotton pants and T-shirts, one red, one yellow. The one who apparently had fallen out sat dripping in a blue suit, white shirt and tie. He wore white stockings and one black shoe. The others wore sandals. They were all looking up at them. We must look like four gargoyles on some old building, Deanie thought.

"What are you doing?" Susan asked.

"We're fishing," Kojo said. He held up a fishing pole and a bait bucket. "We wanted to get an early start, and we thought there would be some flounder under the dock—"

"Some flounder-ing," Barett interrupted.

"Well," Kojo turned to the others in the boat and laughed, "there was an accident, but nothing serious."

"Were you pounding on the deck?" Susan asked.

The oarsman looked up at them, smiled, lifted an oar, pointed it straight up, and thrust it up and down a couple of times.

"I'm glad that's not a spear," Randall said under his breath.

"How did you get here?" Susan asked.

"My friend from Guinea drove his hot rod," Kojo said, extending his hand to the oarsman's shoulder.

"Why don't we all get into a *real* boat?" Randall said as he stood up, rubbing his knees.

Deanie looked to her right and saw the name of their cruiser painted across her stern in gold script: *Island Star*.

*   *   *

"Buoy 42 is out there, and the ferry from Orient Point to New London goes from there to there," the captain said, sweeping his hairy arm from right to left over the wheel, pointing across the sparkling water from the Long Island shore towards Connecticut. Deanie stood next to him and saw the blue and red tattoo on his dark upper arm—a fire-breathing dragon.

He scratched the thick sideburn below his cap where a tuft of silver hair curled over his ear, adjusted the throttle lever, quieting the rumble of the twin diesels, and began wheeling the boat into a gentle turn. He looked back. "Everybody okay back there?" Deanie saw them all leaning out—Kojo and his friends and Randall trolling straight back, while Susan held her rod out to the side and worked it as if she had something on her line. The fellow who had fallen out of the skiff had stripped to the waist and was barefoot. Barett had stuck his rod into a clamp, and was leaning back against the side drinking a beer. He gave a thumbs-up sign and the captain turned back and throttled up.

Deanie looked back at everyone. Kojo had fastened his rod in a clamp and gone over to help Susan with her reel. She felt she had to go back to be with them, but she really enjoyed looking out with the captain. She slid her thumbs back from her chin across her neck and flipped her hair back over her shoulders and started back to where they were fishing. She thought she heard the captain say "Come back," but when she turned she saw that he was resting on the helm, having a cigarette, and blowing a stream of smoke that swirled across the windshield and rolled along the window at his side.

"Did you say something?" she said.

"No," he said, glancing back.

She went down by the others and the wind blew her hair back from her face and she watched the mild trolling wake rolling white into dark blue, and farther out a cruiser and two sailboats glistened white in the glaring sun.

"Aristotle? What the hell does Aristotle have to do with it?" Randall was saying to Kojo. He was holding his rod with both hands as Kojo helped Susan haul up a feisty bluefish. As it came crashing and thrashing to their feet Deanie saw that it was about the size of the one she had caught before she went to check out the captain. She steadied herself on the polished brass rail that ran along the varnished, dark, wood paneling and wondered who had said "Come back." "Nice going, Susan," Randall said. Susan and Kojo worked their hands down the line towards the flopping fish until there were only a few inches left, and the fellow from from Sierra Leone handed Kojo a net, and he slapped it over the fish and stepped on it. The man from Togo reached down with a pair of pliers and, as he had done with everyone else's fish, deftly removed the hook. "So what about Aristotle?"

The fellow from Sierra Leone, in his rolled-up suit pants, lifted the lid of the icebox, and Kojo dropped Susan's fish in with the others. Now everyone had caught at least one bluefish. The fellow from Sierra Leone had caught four, and Kojo's friend from Togo had caught three before Deanie had stopped.

"Aristotle," Kojo said, wiping his hands on a towel, "set the banks for many rivers of thought." He paused and held his hands before his face, touching his finger tips as if he was circumscribing an imaginary globe. "His categories are to a great extent yours."

"Did you see my fish, Deanie?" Susan said, pointing towards the icebox.

"Yes, that was a nice one."

"My second one."

"Super."

"Take Aristotle's example of 'quality,'" Kojo said. Randall shrugged and flexed his rod. "It's 'white,'" Kojo went on.

"'Quality' is 'white.'"

"So?"

"Well, take his example for 'action'—it is 'to cut.'" Kojo slowly dropped his right hand to his back pocket. "'To cut,'" he repeated. "To cut." He seemed to be watching Randall's eyes following his hand. He reached into his pocket, hesitated a moment, and whipped something out towards Randall's startled face and Randall jumped back to slip and fall on his ass. Kojo was holding a ballpoint pen. "Ha!" he laughed, reaching out to help Randall to his feet. "Let's have a beer. You're a good sport, Randall."

"Thanks," Randall said. He turned to fasten his rod in a clamp. "So are you," he said, turning back. His smile looked strained.

Kojo waved the pen at Susan and Deanie. "A beer?"

"Sure," Susan said. "And don't cut yourself with that pen."

"Okay," Deanie said. "I'll have a beer."

Barett was laughing and coughing and clenching his fist in his beard.

"Are you okay?" Deanie asked. He nodded and beckoned her over to his side. She held up a finger to indicate "just a moment," took a beer from Kojo, and picked one out of the cooler for Barett.

"Thanks," Barett said, popping the cap off. "You should have been here a few minutes ago." He wiped his fingers across his cheeks. "I laughed myself to tears. Randall asked Kojo something about the 'culture market' and then Kojo went into a long rap about folklore and ended up giving him a bunch of names and addresses to write down, and when Randall was done writing all the names down Kojo said, 'All of these people are experts in the production of cultures.' And Randall said, 'Production of cultures?' And Kojo said, 'Oh yes, they're the major figures in West African cheese.'" Barett started laughing again.

"Cheese?" she said.

"Cultures—to make cheese." Deanie looked back at Randall and took a swallow of beer. "You should've seen the look on his face," Barett said.

"I wish I had," she said, glad that Kojo had put Randall in his place.

"Seriously," Randall was saying, to Kojo, "seriously—" His voice trailed off and he opened the cooler and began to dig around in the ice. Kojo took a drink of beer, leaned back against the side, and rested his index finger straight up against the front of his goatee. He raised his eyebrows and slid his finger over his lips to rest on his mustache. Deanie recalled how he often took the same pose when listening to students trying to explain something. He looked serious. The fellow from Sierra Leone stepped back from the edge of the boat to listen to Randall. He was as dark as Kojo, though thinner, and a little younger. The two other visitors, working their lines, also looked younger than Kojo, who was about thirty-five, but she realized that it wasn't a difference in age that she was seeing—it was something like attention, or maybe even respect, that seemed to flow from Kojo's companions to him. Whatever it was, it seemed to be present even in the two who were tending their lines. And she realized that, whatever it was, attention or respect, it went both ways; it was something that flowed from Kojo to his friends and back again, though she couldn't tell if it started with him or them. Randall opened his beer and sat on the life jacket trunk. "So much for the culture market," he said, taking a drink. "What about the gold market?"

"What about it?" Kojo said.

He sounded a little defensive to her and when she saw everyone else staring at him she was puzzled. She knew that Ghana produced some gold, that her colonial name had been the Gold Coast—but Randall's remark had stirred something.

Randall took a swallow of beer. "I thought there was gold all over the place," he said.

"Well," Kojo said, "there has been some recent mining development here and there, but definitely not all over the place."

"Come on," Barett said. "Every time they dig a hole, they find gold."

107

"I wasn't aware of that," Kojo said.

"Admit it, Kojo," Barett said, "your being from a noble family"—he paused, extending his fist for emphasis—"you must have gold stashed all over the place."

"Do you think so?" Kojo said, raising his eyebrows and nodding.

"Not to worrry," Barett said, "we won't tell anybody about your gold."

"You're a madman," Kojo said, laughing and nodding his head vigorously.

Randall laughed. "You're a good sport, Kojo. Have a beer."

Hearing that, she told herself that they must have been trying to give Kojo a hard time because Randall had fallen on his ass.

"I think I'll have another beer," Susan said, stretching her legs out from her chair and yawning.

Barett laughed and tossed his empty bottle over his shoulder. "I think I'll have one too."

*   *   *

It was around three-thirty when they got to Kojo's apartment.

"Not bad for a dormitory in the middle of the summer," Randall said, "pretty good air conditioning." Deanie watched him looking at the institutional sofas and chairs that looked like car seats. He walked across the faded, blue rug that covered most of the brown tile floor and stopped to examine the carved wooden figures that rested on the top shelf of a metal bookcase. "And a patio," he said, stepping to his left. He stood a moment by the sliding glass door, then went back to the refrigerator and opened it. "Smells like an Indian restaurant."

"That's curry," Deanie said.

"Love curried chicken," he said. "Hey. Here's some barbecued ribs."

"Those are goat," Susan said.

"Oh," he said. "I'll take a rain check on those. Why don't you order some pizza?"

"Okay, Deanie?" Susan asked.

"Fine with me," she said.

Randall took three green bottles of ale out of the refrigerator, gave one to Susan, set one on the end table by Deanie's chair, and went out to the basketball court where Kojo and two of his visitors and Barett and two black girls who had been sitting on the grass when they drove up were playing half-court. The fellow from Togo was standing at the kitchen sink cleaning the fish.

"Are you going out, Deanie?" Susan asked. She sat across from her watching the game through the patio door. "I can't tell whether they're playing basketball or soccer."

"No, I just feel like sitting here for a while."

The ball flew to one of the visitors. He caught it. Kojo was right next to him. He lifted the ball and headed it to Kojo. One of the girls slapped it down and Kojo's foot shot out to tap it to Barett who pulled it up and turned to meet Randall's hands waving in his face.

"Me too. Barett just doesn't know when to stop."

"How do you mean?" she said, offering Susan a chance to fill her in on anything that had been bothering her.

"He's had enough sun for one day."

"You're probably right," she said, thinking that if anything was bothering Susan about Iris it hadn't built up enough pressure to come out, disguised or otherwise. Deanie heard shouting on the court and looked to see what was going on and the fellow from Togo came over to see. It looked like one of the girls had made a basket. Linda, the grad student Barett had called Kojo's 'resident admirer,' was standing by the court, gleefully clapping her hands over her head. Barett took the ball out of bounds and threw it in. Deanie wondered if the other girls lived there in the graduate dorm, if they were also Kojo's 'resident admirers.'

"How about that basket?" Susan said to the fellow from Togo.

"Okay." He smiled. "Women don't play basketball in Togo."

"I bet they do," she said. He shrugged and went back to the sink.

Watching them all playing, and seeing Linda standing there, Deanie recalled how she and Kojo's teaching assistant had appeared on the court the day she rode by with Barett and Gary, and she began to feel a little short of breath. "How are you doing, Susan. Are you okay?"

Susan knitted her brow and stared. "Deanie? Are *you* okay?"

"What? I'm sorry, I was someplace else." Where had she been? She looked back towards the basketball court. "I don't know, I guess I was just daydreaming or something."

"That's all right," Susan said, "we all have those moments."

Now Linda was walking towards them and Deanie and Susan watched her walking under the maple tree, past the bicycle rack, through the grass towards the patio door. Susan lit a cigarillo, looked around for a place to put her match, and went into the kitchen and from the top cupboard took out a large glass ashtray. She knows where things are, Deanie reflected.

Linda came through the doorway. "Hello," she said. Her eyes sparkled and she looked fresh in her green-plaid cotton dress and sandals.

"Hello," Susan said.

Deanie smiled. "Hi."

"How's the game going?" Susan asked.

"I think they're tied. They're coming up for a break now." The fellow who had been cleaning the fish turned back from the sink. "*Bonjour*," Linda said. He nodded and smiled. "Well," she said, "has the cat got your French tongue?" He mumbled something in French and she waved it off with both hands and looked back towards the players coming from the court. "Is that any way for a chief accountant to talk?" she said. He glanced over his shoulder and shrugged again.

"He's an accountant?" Susan asked.

"Chief Regional Accountant," Linda said, "and his friends—one is a civil engineer and one is a head economist."

"That's impressive," Susan said. She adjusted her blue cotton pullover and sat up a bit as if the presence of Kojo's friends called for more presence on her part, and Deanie watched the others coming in.

After everyone had been inside a few minutes opening beers, mixing drinks, and gulping ice water, Barett started introducing the two young women who had been playing basketball. They were both wearing cut-off jeans and T-shirts. Deanie guessed they were about twenty or twenty-one. He pointed towards the fellow who was cleaning the fish. "And that's Eddie from Tobago."

"Ha!" Kojo laughed.

"*Togo*," Susan said. She looked disgusted.

"Togo, Tobago," Barett said. He smiled and looked around. "Tomay-toe, tomah-toe," he sang, extending his hands palm-up. "You say 'Togo,' I say 'Tobago,'" he went on to the familiar tune, "tomay-toe, tomah-toe, Togo, Tobago—let's fall in love again—"

"Please," Susan said. She looked downcast and appeared to be reading the label on her ale bottle.

Barett looked around at everyone, shrugged, and dropped his hands. "Sorry, everybody. I tried."

Deanie couldn't believe her ears, but, she reflected, there was no way of telling what he had meant.

"A salute to bluefish!" Kojo exclaimed. He raised his glass in a toast and took a drink, and everyone, including Susan, followed suit, and everyone, chatting and laughing, seemed to be in good cheer.

"Do you like it?" Susan said, holding her right hand out towards Deanie, displaying a large gold ring.

"Where did you get that?" she asked.

"I had it in my bag. I didn't want to wear it while we were fishing." She rolled her hand a little, showing the ring's flowered design. "Do you like it?"

111

"Yes," Deanie said, "it's very nice."
"It *is* very nice," Susan said. "I like it a lot."

SEVEN

On her way out of the library Deanie saw the albino-looking guy who'd been sitting at her table in the assigned-reading room bouncing along behind her. She pushed open the door and held it for him.

"Thanks," he said. "Want to get high?"

"No thanks." She threw her book bag over her shoulder.

"That's cool. That's cool," he said, nodding, she thought, excessively.

She was on her way to see Kojo. It had been a couple of weeks since he'd told her that he'd tell her what was troubling him about Susan and she just couldn't wait any longer.

Deanie parked in the street and cut across the grass towards Kojo's patio, glad that nobody was playing basketball. As she came up to the patio door she could see Kojo sitting at his kitchen table. He was wearing a tan polo shirt and appeared to be peeling potatoes. She flipped her hair back over her shoulders and knocked on the glass. Kojo got up and on his way to the door turned on the patio light. She looked at her reflection in the glass, tugged the edge of her sleeveless blouse towards her shoulder, straightened up a bit, and stuck her hands in her back pockets.

"Deanie," he said, "come in, come in. What brings you here?"

"I just thought I'd say hello. I had some articles to read at the library, so I was passing by. Unless you're busy." She went in.

"I'm not too busy for you." He gestured with his hand. "Come. Sit down."

She followed him to the kitchen. "What smells so good?"

"A friend just brought me some guava jelly tarts."

"Was it Linda?" Deanie said.

"Oh, yes. I think she's trying to make me fat." He laughed, and pointed to the counter where a tray of five tarts sat cooling. She gripped her jeans to keep from grabbing one. "Please have one."

She took one. "This is delicious," she said. "Where did she get the guava jelly?"

"She made it at home on St. Croix."

"She has some real domestic talents."

His eyes opened wide, and, nodding in agreement, he leaned over as if confiding to her in a crowded room. "She does—and if she had her way, she would preserve *me* and take me back with her on the plane."

"She really would?"

"Yes—that's just between you and me." He chuckled and took a pitcher of iced tea out of the refrigerator. "Want some?"

"Please." He poured two tall glasses. "That's quite a compliment," she said.

"It is. But that's not where I'm *at*, as they say."

"Where *are* you," she paused, "at?"

"Where am I *at*?" He laughed and took a drink of his iced tea. "Would you like some lemon?"

"This is fine." She pulled a chair out and sat at the round table. She saw the knife, the carved block of wood, and the wood chips brushed into a pile in the center of the table. "I thought you were peeling potatoes." He looked puzzled. "From the patio—it looked like you were peeling potatoes."

"Oh," he said. "I still do a little wood carving sometimes when I'm thinking."

"Thinking about where you're at?" she said. He laughed and sat at the table. "Or thinking about how you're going to get back whatever it is Susan has?"

"Deanie, you're too much." He paused, running his thumb through the condensation on his glass. "How do you know Susan has still got it—whatever *it* is?"

"Well, I haven't seen you around for a while and Susan hasn't had much to say lately."

"What can you conclude from that?"

"Nothing—which is why I was sort of wondering—as a friend..." she said, pausing.

"What's going on?" he said. "Maybe Susan has some old love letters that I want back?" He raised his eyebrows and nodded.

"People don't write love letters any more—at least I don't get any."

He laughed. "I assure you, people still write love letters. One of these days I'll send you one."

"That's sweet of you." He looked serious, conciliatory almost, as though he felt that he really owed her a love letter. She sipped her tea.

"Tell me," he said, "how have your parents been? How is your mother doing?"

"My mother sounds a lot better on the phone. She joined a support group of women with similar problems, so at least she won't feel so alone when I go to Naples."

"That's good."

115

"My dad's okay. He got to sit in with some guys from a big band after a concert a couple of weeks ago. He was really thrilled about that."

"I know the feeling. I was once fortunate enough to play drums with Bud Powell's group in Paris, and I'll never forget it."

"Bud Powell!" she shouted. "Are you kidding me?"

"Not at all," he said. "I played my *husago* and *brekete* drums."

"Your ritual drums—bigger than bongoes, smaller than congas?" He nodded. "The ones you brought to class?"

"That's right—I did. And I believe that was when one of the students said you would be glad to accompany me on the piano."

"Somebody said that?"

"You do play, don't you?"

"I like to, but I haven't been able to play very often. There's an old upright in the Burkharts' apartment, but it's out of tune."

"What's out of tune—the piano or Burkharts' apartment?"

"Well, actually, both. Which brings us back to what Susan has of yours."

Kojo picked up the piece of wood and turned it in his hands, silently. She watched him roll it and turn it. He took the knife and curled a thin shaving off the side. He rubbed the wood with his thumb. "I'll tell you about my wood carving, and then maybe you'll understand in a general way where I'm at. And then perhaps you can see how Susan fits in. Or as you already sense, doesn't fit in." He got up and switched off the patio light. "Some people take my patio light as a beacon—if it's on they try to come in and bullshit at all hours of the night." He sat down and picked up the piece of wood. "I began to"—he paused—"I got my first glimpses of the inner life of things when"—he paused—"around the age of seven I began to spend a lot of time with an uncle by the name of Vinoko Ekpe."

"I remember seeing his picture when you invited the class over," she said.

"That's right—" he said, "this one." He slid the picture from an envelope of pictures and clippings that had been lying on the table. "His daughter mailed it to me last spring to let me know that he's in good health. He's seventy-five now."

"He doesn't look that old," she said. Deanie studied the black and white photograph. It was a head and shoulders picture of a man whose brow and cheek bones seemed to actually give attention to his eyes, eyes that seemed to look just a little above the camera. He wore a dashiki and had some sort of garment draped over his shoulder. "When was this taken?"

"That was taken on his birthday last spring. And here's a picture of Dr. Nkrumah." He handed her another black and white photograph. "That's Dr. Nkrumah," he said, pointing to a man behind a podium in front of several rows of young men and women who appeared to be in school uniforms. "And there I am, first row, fourth one in."

She glanced up to compare Kojo's face with the younger one in the photograph and looking back saw the newspaper clipping about the former Ghanaian president's death back in April. She held the picture up. "You must have been a student here," she said.

"Oh, yes," he said, taking the pictures and the clipping, and putting them back in the envelope, "definitely." He took a drink. "In any case, my first memories of Vinoko Ekpe are as a storyteller. No—that's not quite right. As a voice telling a story. His voice was rich with stories of extraordinary deeds and high adventures." His mention of adventures brought a smile to her face, and she recalled, for a moment, walking along a beach somewhere at sunrise. "Many afternoons I sat alone or with other children listening to him tell about rescuing the unwary from fierce crocodiles, hunting marvelous birds with catapults, and sending brave soldiers against those who made war against the village.

"I think Vinoko's greatest influence was in teaching me how to carve wood. Wood carving as such is not a tradition with the Ewe—as it is with, say, the Ashanti—so when he showed me what he had learned on his travels I was fascinated."

She thought she'd heard him give his tribal name a new pronunciation. "You're an"—she inwardly checked it—*ay-vay*—"you're an *Ewe*? Did I get it right?"

He frowned and nodded. "That's pretty close."

"I just thought I heard something else." Deanie tapped her ear and hoped she wasn't blushing. Whatever had caused her moment of uncertainty had passed.

"So," he said, "over the years, till I went away to the university, I spent a lot of time learning about carving from Vinoko. At first I learned how to sharpen and care for our carving tools. Then gradually I learned how to handle the wood, determine densities, and get a feel for how the grain was running. When I started carving small objects—geometric forms, crocodiles, faces—I learned how to look for the figure that was already in the wood." He paused and examined the piece of wood. "Then the task was to cut away the unnecessary parts.

"I remember Vinoko going off to England when I was a boy. He went to attend what I subsequently learned was the Pan-Africanist Conference in Manchester. At the time his trip was a big deal for me because he had designated me keeper of the tools." Kojo held the thin, long-handled knife straight up on the table and twisted it between his thumb and forefinger. As he twisted it back and forth the blade flashed in the light. "It seemed that he was gone for a long time. I remember starting a letter to him, but I put it aside when my teacher told me that he was on his way home.

"He brought me a gift—a piece of the hard, white *osese* wood that the Ashanti use in making their carved stools. One of the delegates to the conference had brought some of the wood for a display on Ashanti stool carving at the Museum of African Art in London, and Vinoko got a piece from him. When he gave it to me he said that his getting the *osese* wood in England should remind me of how owing to colonialist practices so many African things can't be gotten in Africa by Africans.

"As time passed Vinoko showed me how his carving helped him to meditate. Little by little his thoughts flowed more and more into talk of 'unity' and 'higher purpose' beyond 'boundaries scratched in the dirt.' As he spoke of how to live, he spoke of being faithful to the grain, of examining knots and imperfections to see if they couldn't be incorporated into the overall design. If you had to remove something by cutting directly across the grain, you should examine your cutting edges, and then move with steady, sustained pressure. And you should not position yourself in such a way that if the tool were to slip you would cut your own flesh."

Kojo leaned back and stretched his arms behind his head. "Then when I was fourteen Vinoko took me to the grasslands and taught me how to shoot his old Lee-Enfield .303 carbine. The stocks on those carbines were a little short, and every so often, when I wasn't holding mine properly, the recoil would drive my thumb back into my nose and make it bleed." He held his fist up and tapped his nose with his thumb. "But before too long I learned how to handle it and I became a pretty good shot. That particular gun had been used against the German army in West Africa, and I found that fascinating—and then Vinoko told me that it was the British who first used concentration camps to hold a civilian population. That was during the Boer War in South Africa."

Kojo leaned forward and rested his arms on the table. He picked up the piece of wood and the knife, examined them, and set them back. He started moving the shavings around with his finger. "Once I was at the university my carving became something that I did less and less, and then hardly at all. But the principles I learned from Vinoko stayed with me. And I remember when I came across Michaelangelo's comments about the sculptor revealing the figure that is already in the block of marble—I could see how in a way Vinoko Ekpe and I were on the same track, trying to see how to develop new forms of democracy from African culture, trying to show how the search for viable forms of democracy is truly an artistic search. Using science, of course—as one might develop tools to use in a larger enterprise.

"And I keep up the search, looking for forms that will lead to the end of betrayals—intra-national and personal. And this looking almost got me shot."

Deanie straightened up and clasped her hands under her chin. "How?"

"It was about six years ago when I was working with a film crew in a remote part of Ghana. Essentially I was in the wrong place at the wrong time. That was after I had been teaching in the university for quite a while and working with various film crews on an occasional basis. After that I went back to London where I met Susan the next summer."

He sat still a moment, slid the knife in front of him, and, holding it with his thumb and middle finger, snapped it to spin around and around. He watched it spinning and slowing to a stop. He spun it again, and without looking up watched it come to a stop. Gradually the table began swelling in circumference, and Deanie began seeing spirits sitting around it. Kojo spun the knife again and again. It was as if he was engaged in a variation of spin-the-bottle, waiting to see what spirit sitting around the table would be selected for some form of communication. Some of the spirits were familiar—she had seen pictures of their persons. Some were unfamiliar—she had only heard Kojo speak of them. There was Vinoko Ekpe, and there was Kwame Nkrumah, and there was Kojo's father—no, it was Eshu-Elegba, the trickster-god, smiling and gesturing. There was a black soldier, an American, his face covered with bandages. There was Anyievo, the rainbow god. There was Kojo's father, and So, the god of thunder, and Michael Harper, the poet—no, it was Ho Chi Minh, no, it was the trickster-god. Maybe they were all just manifestations of the trickster-god. The knife was pointing towards her.

"What have you got to say?" Kojo said, resting his arms on the table.

The question startled her. Now she didn't see any spirits. Only she and Kojo were at the table. "Well—" She paused. He had done so much and was so full of promise. She didn't know what to say. She took a breath and reached across the table. "The mojo hand," she said, resting her hand on his. She laughed a little. "No," she said. "It's the Kojo hand."

Kojo laughed. "I believe it is," he said.

"I'm really touched that you've told me all of this," she said, remembering why she'd come to visit him. "But maybe if you told me what it is that Susan has, maybe I could help you. Unless..."

"Unless what?"

"Unless I think Susan's the one who needs help." He laughed. "Or if it's something like piece of jewelry that you want back, I wouldn't pay any attention to it," she said.

"A piece of jewelry?" He laughed. "That's very funny," he said. "You must be careful. You're starting to sound like Barett."

"Pardon me?" she said, annoyed at the comparison.

Kojo laughed. "Not to worry. Come. Let's go." He brushed the wood shavings off the table into his hand, got up, and dropped them into a garbage can under the sink. "Let's go out to the Shamrock for a drink."

"Okay, but let's both drive so I can go straight home afterwards."

"Good idea," he said. "Do you have exams Friday?"

"History."

"And your instructor won't want brandied history."

"I don't think so. We'll save that for Saturday. You are coming out to Iris's Saturday afternoon, aren't you?"

"I think so. Iris called this afternoon and said she was having a few people over for a barbecue." He clicked on the patio light, walked around the waist-high partition into the living room, and turned to wait for her.

"Are you going to tell me what it is of yours that Susan has?" she said. "I really have to know."

121

Kojo clasped his hands, and, resting his extended forefingers on his goatee, looked into her eyes, the look on his face gradually softening. "You have to know?" She nodded. "Okay," he said, "if Susan doesn't bring what I want to Iris's barbecue, I'll tell you what it is, and then maybe you can help me get it."

"Is that a condition for telling me?"

His eyes narrowed a moment, and his lips puckered as if he was going to whistle. "No."

EIGHT

Now after a morning of hitting the books and studying her Italian, Deanie was on her way to Iris's place to see Kojo and her friends. She walked along the old bridle path that ran past Zerk's pits and curved down to Iris's yard, and looking ahead she could see how truck tires had crushed tracks in the blue-green weeds along either side of the path.

As the path opened into the clearing she could hear a truck idling and now she could see the tank truck parked on the opposite side of the second pit in the row of four that ran back into the clearing. A large hose from the back of the tank lay over the edge of the pit, spilling a dark gray liquid down the gravel. The truck driver, wearing steel-rimmed glasses and a wrinkled canvas hat, stood by the hose, smoking a cigarette.

"Hey, Deanie," Zerk shouted from across the clearing. He was waving at her. "Just a minute."

Deanie waved and watched him climb into the red cab of the crane, start the engine, lower the boom, and haul up a drag bucket that was shaped like a huge sardine can with the end cut off. When the bucket was off the ground he shut off the engine, came out of the cab, sidled along the edge of the truck bed to its cab, climbed in, started the engine, and began moving the whole thing towards her, along the oval track past the tank truck.

"He can really handle that," the truck driver said.

"He grew up with heavy equipment," she said.

"It looks like it," he said as they watched the truck crane rumbling towards them.

When the boom was a car length from the truck, Zerk shut off the engine and jumped down. The truck driver rolled up the last section of hose at the rear of his truck, climbed into his seat, and backed away. Zerk waved good-bye to him and threw his arms out to greet her.

"I was wondering when you'd get here," he said, throwing his arms around her.

She slid her hands over his shoulders and watching his eyes close felt his kiss and now, eyes closed, she felt him closer and warmer and stronger and gentler and all around her.

"So," he was saying, "what have you been doing all morning?"

She looked at him now, standing there, his hands on her arms.

"I've been studying," she said. She smiled and flipped her hair over her shoulders. *"Ci sono dei soldati vicini?"*

Zerk stared at her. "So?" he said.

"Are there soldiers near here?" she said, looking around playfully.

He put his hands on his hips. "Well, there's one," he paused, "one ex-soldier here."

Deanie straightened her shirt and adjusted her bracelets. "Well then, *portatemi della cioccolata.*"

"What?"

"Bring me chocolate."

He tried to look serious and checked the pockets of his jeans. "I just might have some chocolate in the cab of my crane," he said, reaching out and taking her hand.

"You think so?"

"Something sweet," he said, leading her to the crane. She knew what he had in mind and she tried to look askance as he smiled over his shoulder, but she couldn't help smiling back.

At the side of the truck he locked his hands together and bent down so she could step up for a boost.

"You won't drop me?" she said.

"No way," he said.

Deanie stepped into his hands and rested her hands on his shoulders. "Okay," she said, feeling his shoulder muscles ripple, and up she went coming to rest on the bed of the truck, her legs dangling and now tight against Zerk's ribs as he pushed her shirt up with his head and now kissed and nibbled her stomach and slid his hands up and around her waist and she slid her hands along his arms and across his shoulders. "Let's get in the truck," she said, patting his shoulders, and she felt him lifting her and turning towards the cab, now setting her on the edge of the seat and unbuttoning her jeans.

*   *   *

It was still early afternoon when Deanie and Zerk came out of the woods and into Iris's yard. A few people were trying to play basketball and a few were hanging out in the yard. Now Deanie and Zerk were in the basketball game and as the ball flew above the garage roofline Deanie lost it in the sun. Now Zerk had it, stepping back to the edge of the concrete apron. She turned, stepped, and went up with him, reaching. Her fingers brushed the ball and her hand chopped Zerk's shoulder and slid down his damp hair and across his sweaty arm, and she stumbled onto the grass to see the ball go up again, arc into the edge of the backboard, spin off the doorframe, and bounce out to Barett.

125

"Set it up," Barett shouted. He held the ball over his head, away from Linda's waving arms.

"Over here," Kojo said. His beckoning hands signaled for the ball behind Terence. Barett flipped the ball. Linda snatched it. Terence and Zerk closed on her. She went up for a jump shot. Zerk stretched up behind her, punched the ball free, and Terence, off balance, slipped, and smashed it through the doorway to slam the metal garbage can lid into Iris's motorcycle. Albert barked and tugged his rope.

"Hey," Iris shouted from the porch steps. "Watch out for my bike."

Gary stood by the picnic table, resting his leg on the crossbar of his bicycle. Susan sat next to him, smoking a cigarillo.

Deanie pushed Zerk's sweat from her upper arm, wiped her forearm on her jeans, and drew the top of her forearm across her cheek and under her nose. The slight scent of sweat and clover and wild flowers smelled good.

"Gonna call you Hatchet Hand," Zerk said, coming back. He clasped his shoulder and moved his extended arm in a circle, as if checking for muscle damage.

"Sorry." She lifted her ponytail from her neck, flipped it back, and pulled her T-shirt out from her chest a few times to let the air circulate.

As Zerk stepped back onto the concrete slab Terence fired the ball to him and he caught it chest-high.

"You heal fast," Deanie said, flipping her shirt up to cool her stomach.

"I have to." He faked a throw to her and fired the ball to Terence who threw his hand out, smacking Kojo in the face with a sharp crack. The ball landed on the grass and Kojo covered his nose with his hand. Now he was looking into his hand, and Deanie saw the blood dripping off his mustache.

"Get a wet washcloth," she called to Iris. Iris turned and ran to the kitchen.

"Jeez, I'm sorry," Terence said, standing in front of Kojo, his hands up as if he were pleading for mercy.

126

"That's all right," Kojo said, "it's nothing."

"Here's a handkerchief," Zerk said. "It's clean." He handed his handkerchief to Kojo. "How does it feel?"

"It's all right," Kojo said, taking the handkerchief. "Thank you."

"Do you feel dizzy?" Deanie asked.

"No, I'll be all right."

"You're sure?"

"Yes, I'm quite sure. I'm okay."

"That's good." She was relieved to hear that.

"It'll be all right," Kojo said. He readjusted the handkerchief on his nose. "It'll be all right. I'll go put a cold cloth on it."

"Tip your head back," Zerk said.

"I know. Not to worry. I was telling Deanie a while back that I used to get a bloody nose from time to time firing an old Lee-Enfield. It's nothing. I'll put a damp cloth on it, and that will be it."

"You shoot a Lee-Enfield?" Zerk said.

"I used to practice with one," Kojo said, glancing at Deanie, "a long time ago." Kojo tipped his head back, and holding the handkerchief to his nose, started across the lawn towards the house. Gary was wide-eyed. Susan moved her hands to her knees as if she contemplated getting up.

Zerk took a couple of steps after him. "I've got a little range set up out in back. We can go blow up some paper after you get your nose taken care of," Zerk said. "It'll be a lot safer than our so-called basketball game."

"Blow up some paper?" Kojo, said, looking back. He laughed, checked the handkerchief, and put it back to his nose. "All right, we'll blow up some paper." He continued on to the house, his muscular thighs stretching the white tennis shorts. Gary rode his bicycle along behind him, the front wheel wobbling and twisting over the bumpy lawn, and behind Gary went Linda, brushing the seat and sides of her new jeans. Iris came onto the porch and held the screen door open.

*   *   *

Looking ahead, Deanie watched a white butterfly skimming over the weeds along the old bridle path. Zerk was walking next to her, carrying a .22 rifle at his side. He had a pistol stuck inside his jeans, and his faded blue T-shirt was tucked in behind it. Kojo was next to him on the path. He was carrying an old double-barreled shotgun that Zerk had brought up from Iris's basement. Kojo's muscles filled the sleeve of his white polo shirt and seemed to throb as if he was squeezing the stock of the gun every few steps. Deanie was carrying a canvas bag of ammo and earplugs. Linda and Susan trailed Kojo, each with a handful of paper targets. Several yards back, Terence brought up the rear. He had put his western hat back on after the basketball workout, and he was batting milkweed pods with a stick.

"There's our range," Zerk said, pointing towards a long narrow pit that had dirt piled up along the edge on one side and then across the edge of the far end.

Zerk stopped on the oval track and turned around. "Is anybody else coming?"

"Iris is working on her motorcycle," Deanie said, as the others came up to them.

"Barett stayed with Gary," Susan said.

"What about Albert?" Zerk said. "We want to account for everybody."

Terence swung at a white butterfly. "He's tied up."

"I'm going to move the crane out of the way," Zerk said. He started to hand the rifle to Linda, but Susan put her hand out and he gave it to her. "It's not loaded, but treat it like it is. Just keep it pointed at the ground."

He ran back between the four square pits and a long row of concrete drainpipes stretched end-to-end along the newly dug, narrow pit that was about twenty or thirty yards long. They all seemed to be watching Zerk moving the truck-crane.

Zerk jumped down from the cab and started back towards them.

"Hey, Kojo, you ought to take him and his crane home with you to build bridges," Terence said.

"We need people to *be* bridges," Kojo said.

Zerk's cigarettes popped out of his shirtsleeve, and he stopped to pivot and scoop them up, his long hair swinging down, covering his face. On the upswing he picked up a rock the size of a softball, and, in the motion of a shot-putter, threw it out to splash in the pit next to him. He raised his arm in a victory sign and came up to them.

"That sounds deep," Terence said.

"Could be ten feet," Zerk said, "more or less. There must be some clay holding the water. Maybe a little spring in there someplace."

*   *   *

"Looks good, Linda," Zerk said, coming back with her target. Deanie watched him walking back along the center of the long, narrow pit. "Three out of five on the paper. Are you sure you haven't shot before?"

"As I said, just a BB gun at carnival." She laid the .22 on a waist-high bench made of two-by-fours that Zerk had put near the middle of the pit. She adjusted the sleeves of her shirt and came back past the bench.

"Terence," Zerk said, "Deanie needs a target. Would you put one up?"

Terence jogged to the end of the pit where Zerk had been tacking targets on a four-by-eight sheet of drywall that stood up against the big pile of dirt. Terence had shot first, demonstrating the earplugs, the sight picture, aiming the rifle, and pointing the shotgun while Zerk described them. Terence jogged back, came around the bench, and stood with Deanie, Kojo, Linda, and Susan. Zerk took the magazine out of the .22 and loaded five rounds—a term Deanie had just learned from him.

129

"Come on, Hatchet Hand, you're next," Zerk said. He stood back against the side of the pit, his elbow loosening some sand to trickle down and settle behind the heel of his oiled, leather work boots.

Deanie moved towards Zerk, and Linda came away from the bench to let her by. "Hatchet Hand?" Linda said.

"She nearly broke my collarbone playing basketball," Zerk said.

"Good luck," Linda said, backing next to Susan.

"Was that for me or Deanie?" Zerk asked.

"Both of you," Linda said.

"I know, Linda," he said, smiling, "thanks." He adjusted his green headband. "Do you want to use the rifle, or should I just put a round on the bench and let you fire it with a karate chop?" Kojo laughed and Terence moved closer to Susan and Linda.

"I'd rather shoot the shotgun," Deanie said.

"Okay," Zerk said. "Have you ever shot one?"

"I shot my uncle's goose gun out at his dairy farm."

"What were you doing? Chasing the cows around to make whipped cream?" he said.

Deanie rolled her eyes, broke open the shotgun, picked two shells from the table, and slid them in.

Zerk held up a pair of earplugs. "Okay, everybody, time for these if you don't have 'em in yet." Deanie put the gun down, put in the plugs, then picked it up, and closed it. "Okay?" Zerk said.

She knew that with the earplugs you could still hear talking, but not as much of the bang. The plugs felt comfortable. She nodded. "Okay," she said.

Zerk leaned over to check the shotgun. "And don't forget the safety," he said.

Deanie nodded and Zerk backed away. Looking to her left, she lined herself up with the target, slid her feet apart for support, pulled the stock tight into her shoulder, switched off the safety, pressed her cheek against her thumb, and looked down the barrels at the target.

"Is the safety off?" She nodded. "Have you got the front trigger?" She nodded again. "Go ahead," Zerk said. She remembered for a moment shooting the coffee cans at her uncle's farm.

She fired, felt the jolt. Dust rolled out from around the target.

"That's *loud*," Linda exclaimed.

Deanie laid the shotgun on the bench and rubbed the front of her shoulder.

"How's the shoulder?" Zerk asked.

"Fine." She could feel where it had jolted, but it didn't hurt.

"Want to shoot again?"

"No," she said, "somebody else can. I'll go put up another target." Walking towards the end of the pit, she looked up at a flock of starlings swirling overhead. Along the right side Zerk had piled the dirt from the pit, and every so often above the weeds on the left side she could see the top of one of the tiles that he had strung out as part of his so-called training layout. The pattern of shot had torn up the paper target and spread fairly evenly, she thought, around it on the drywall.

When she got back to the bench Kojo was getting ready to shoot Zerk's pistol, a Government Model Colt .45. She stood back with the others and watched him holding it out with both hands, firing, rising with recoil, dropping-aiming-firing, rising with recoil, dropping-aiming-firing.

"That's *loud*," Linda said.

"That's the real thing," Zerk said. "Not like TV."

The real thing, Deanie thought. There it was again. That phrase Randall had used at her first modeling session. It bothered her, and she didn't want to think about it.

Kojo was firing the pistol—from the recoiled lift, dropping-aiming-firing; from the recoiled lift, dropping-aiming-firing...

"Let me get the target," Zerk said. Kojo put the pistol down, and Zerk went after the target. He put up another one, brought Kojo's back, and put it on the bench. "Not bad. About a seven-inch group. Not bad at all. Are you that good with a blowgun?"

"We just make those to sell to tourists," Kojo said, "but watch out for my spear."

"Can I shoot it?" Susan asked. She stepped between Deanie and Linda and stood next to Kojo.

"Wouldn't you rather shoot the .22?" Zerk asked.

"Is it legal to shoot back here?" Linda asked.

"Shotgun's okay five hundred feet from a building," Zerk said. "But if somebody actually came all the way back here, we'd have to pretend that we were only shooting the shotgun, or training on my .30 caliber cement-nail gun." He reached to a shelf under the bench, pulled out what must have been the nail gun, and held it up. "You load a .30 caliber cartridge, hold it like a staple gun, and it shoots nails. Very loud," he said, as he put it back under the bench, "or at least loud enough for nosey neighbors."

"Let me shoot the pistol," Susan said, pointing at the .45.

"Okay," Zerk said. "Are you through, Kojo?"

"Yes. Go ahead," Kojo said. He stepped back and stood by Deanie.

"Have you ever shot a .45?" Zerk asked.

"No, but I want to learn," Susan said.

"All right," Zerk said. "I loaded five rounds, so there's one in the chamber, and four in the—"

"Magazine."

"Right. You learn fast." He moved close behind her, reached around her shoulders and held the pistol up so she could grasp it with both hands. He wrapped his hands around hers. "Let's try one together. Are you ready?" She nodded. Their hands went up together. "Sight picture okay?" She nodded. "Squeeze the trigger." The pistol fired. "Fine. Now you do it." He slid his hands along her forearms and backed away.

Susan rested the muzzle on the bench, took a breath, and lifted the pistol to aim.

Deanie thought she saw him first, with the little yellow bucket and the big blue spoon, coming around the dirt piled above the target. Her warning caught in her throat when she saw

132

Kojo reach out and tap Zerks's arm and nod towards Gary. Zerk raised his hand to keep everyone still.

"Look at the bench, Susan," Zerk said firmly and calmly.

Susan looked at the bench and the heavy pistol came down a few inches. "How come?" she said.

"It's important to keep looking at the bench, and put the pistol down right on the bench," Zerk said.

She's not going to shoot, Deanie thought. Now, just so Gary doesn't fall. Susan put the pistol down and Gary slid on the dirt and came feet first down the drywall as if it had been a playground slide.

"Watch out!" Linda screamed.

Susan looked up. "Oh my god!" she screamed. "My baby!"

*   *   *

Deanie sat with her elbows on the picnic table, resting her chin in her hands. She was looking between Zerk and Linda, sitting across from her, and watching Susan and Barett, sitting on the glider on the porch. "I wonder what they're talking about?" Deanie said to no one in particular.

"Susan's already asked how on earth he could have let Gary go back to the pits," Zerk said. He sat at the end of the table, leaning back in a lawn chair. "Now Barett's probably explaining how he had to go in to the bathroom, or how he had to help Iris with the motorcycle for just a minute, or—" He shrugged and took a drink of his beer.

"Lucky you got back here first," Terence said to Zerk from the other end of the table.

"He was in the house with Iris?" Linda asked.

Zerk nodded.

Kojo sat next to Deanie, sipping his drink. "How did you know where they were?"

"Nobody was in the garage, so I figured they were in the house," Zerk said.

"What'd you do then?" Terence asked.

133

"I just went up and hollered through the screen door that Gary had been trying to play target back at the range, and that Susan was on her way back to the house with him and would probably want to see Barett." Zerk finished his beer, crumpled the can in his hand, and belched.

"Susan was awfully anxious to learn how to shoot your pistol," Terence said. He sat back in his lawn chair, a smug smile growing in the shadow of his bushy mustache.

"She didn't come here to shoot," Zerk said. "I didn't even know we were going to the range until just before we went. And, in any case, you and Iris are the only ones who knew I had a .45."

"Susan's no doormat," Terence said. "I don't think she was ever one to sit in her room and sulk." He took a sip of wine, and looked at Linda as if he were passing a ball in a game.

"You know," Zerk said, "Barett's not a doormat either." He paused. "Maybe Susan's doing something that makes *him* feel bad, and Iris happens to be the one who makes him feel better."

"What do you mean 'doing something'?" Deanie asked.

"It's hard to say," Zerk said. He popped open another can of beer. "Maybe she's spending a lot of time with somebody, or engaged in something she doesn't want to talk about. That could make a spouse feel bad. Right, Kojo?"

"I think there are cultural dimensions to your question," Kojo said, smiling. "But why ask me?"

"You're a man of the world—international affairs, limousines, books, political issues—"

"Ha!" Kojo laughed. "Perhaps if I knew what you think I am supposed to know, I wouldn't be sitting here," Kojo said, "but don't take that personally."

"No problem, my man," Zerk said. He lifted his drink in a toast. "To your sharp-eyed action at the range," he said, taking a drink.

Kojo nodded. "And to yours," he said, and he finished his drink.

"Thank you," Zerk said. "And now if you'll excuse me, I'm going to go light the charcoal so we can cook those big steaks that Susan and Barett brought." He stood up, stretched, and tipped his beer can up to drain it.

*   *   *

Now it was nearly dark and Iris's guests were getting ready to leave—picking up coolers and badminton rackets and loading their cars. Iris and Kojo were standing by the porch and Barett and Gary were walking towards Susan, who was opening the gate on their station wagon. Two carloads of people, yelling and honking, bounced down the driveway and squealed their tires up the road. Suddenly it seemed abysmally quiet and Deanie felt the edge of darkness cutting through the yard like a slow-moving icebreaker cracking a sheet of green ice. The August heat was still there, but it seemed internal, separate from the surfaces of the grass, the trees, the white clapboard house shading to gray.

It was only nine o'clock, and yet everyone seemed to be leaving. It all felt really strange and Deanie took Zerk's hand for comfort. It was as though some feeling or feelings had become embodied in the icebreaker of night, and as it slid towards the west it cracked all of them apart from each other and left each of them standing on a little green patch of ice—some floating towards the house, some floating towards the parked cars.

Susan was having trouble getting the gate on the station wagon open.

"Come on," Deanie said, heading for Susan.

Zerk nodded and gave her hand a little squeeze.

"Do you need a hand, Susan?" Deanie asked.

"No, I'll get it," Susan snapped. Susan tugged at the partially open gate, hit it with her fist, and it fell open. "But," she sighed, pointing to Gary's bike lying in the grass, "I could use some help with that."

Zerk picked up the bike and set it on the gate.

135

"Thanks," she said, "I'll finish this." She shoved the bike into the station wagon until it jammed against Barett's golf clubs. "Shit."

"I'm going to get a beer," Zerk said. "Do you want one, Deanie?"

"Not now," she said. She was about to ask Susan if she wanted any help, but stopped when she saw the determination in Susan's face. "Does Barett still golf?" Deanie asked.

"No," Susan said, twisting the bike. "He keeps this bag of clubs here for when a cop stops him for weaving." She shoved the bike and it went all the way in past the clubs. "He points to the clubs and says something cute about the nineteenth hole and the cop lets him go without a ticket."

"Really?"

"Always. At least when I've been with him. But there are a lot of things he doesn't want to tell me about. Right, Iris?"

Deanie turned to see Iris standing there wide-eyed, holding the Burkharts' cooler.

"Right what?" Iris said.

"Nothing," Susan said. "It doesn't really concern you anyhow. You're just"—she paused—"you're just there."

"I don't get it," Iris said.

"Never mind," Susan said.

"I brought your cooler."

"Thanks."

Iris looked from Deanie to Susan to Deanie and back to Susan. "Safe home."

"Thanks."

She started away and turned back. "By the way, you're coming to Zerk's birthday party, aren't you? He'll be thirty. I'm hoping it'll be a surprise." She put her finger to her lips.

"I'll be here," Susan said.

Deanie went towards the house to see if Kojo had gotten what he'd wanted from Susan.

Iris stopped halfway to let her catch up. "Just a second," she said. "Was Susan talking about me when I brought the cooler down?"

"Sort of," Deanie said. "She's upset about whatever she thinks is going on between you and Barett. You must know that?"

"I guess so. But to hear Barett, it's a case of the pot calling the kettle hot. I mean she's been spending a lot of time with Kojo for a long time, and Barett can't take it anymore."

"Don't get me wrong, I'm not telling you what to do or not to do, but I think Barett's imagining a lot," Deanie said. "A whole lot."

"I can't talk now," Iris said. "Why don't you stop by the Shamrock tomorrow night. I'll be tending bar, so you can sit at the bar, and we can talk, and I'll just charge you for your first drink." She winked.

"All right. But if I can't get a car, I'll probably have to come with somebody."

"That's okay. Your friends are my friends." Iris reached out and Deanie clasped her hand.

"Susan's my friend," Deanie said.

Iris smiled. "I know," she said, sighing and shrugging.

At the picnic table, Iris took a steak bone from a paper plate and carried it back to Albert. Kojo was sitting at the table, clicking a flashlight on and off. He watched Deanie sit down and nodded a greeting.

"Hello," Deanie said. She glanced around and leaned over to him. "Did you get what you wanted from Susan?"

He shook his head. "Not yet."

"What is it? I want to help."

Kojo sighed. "Can you come over to my place in a half hour?"

"I think I can work it out," she said. "I'll borrow Zerk's car."

Going back towards the bridle path, Deanie noticed that Barett's station wagon was still parked on the edge of the

137

grass—Barett stood behind it, tapping on the taillight lens with a screwdriver. Susan's window was down and her head rested back on the seat as if she was sleeping. Gary sat next to her, hitting the rear-view mirror with a fly swatter. Deanie wondered if he could see his father's reflection in the mirror. She stopped by Barett. "Is something wrong?"

He snorted and sighed. "Do you want the short answer or the long one?"

"The short one."

"The bulb was loose, and I fixed it."

"That's good." She stepped away. "I have to go now. Good night." After about five steps she realized that Barett was right behind her, and she stopped.

"I don't know what you know," he said, "and I'm not going to put you on the spot now by asking. But I want you to know that I'm going to find out what Dedu is really up to—and that includes his affair with Susan."

"Affair?"

"Whatever you want to call it."

"But I don't know what"—he cut her off with a wave of his hand, and mumbling something she didn't catch, he turned away—"you're talking about."

*   *   *

The fluorescent kitchen light made the silvery pearl table top vibrate where it met the outline of Kojo's arms. And what Barett had said about Kojo's "affair" with Susan and finding out what Kojo was "really" up to made Deanie feel like her head was vibrating too.

She had been in Kojo's apartment for only a few minutes, just long enough to pour a glass of wine and sit down, but the silence in the apartment and the vibrations inside her made it seem like she'd been there for a long time.

Kojo sat there running his finger around the rim of his glass. Deanie had never known him to be depressed. She had seen him tired. She had seen him quiet. Now he looked a little more than tired, and as the silence went on he seemed to sink into himself. He looked depressed. She looked around the waist-high partition that separated the dining area from the living room and saw Linda coming in. Deanie waved and beckoned her to the table.

Linda came to the table. "Good evening," she said, nodding to both of them.

"Hello," Deanie said.

Kojo nodded.

Linda stood there a moment and then poured herself a glass of wine. "Kojo has forgotten to toast his ancestors," she said. Kojo looked up. "Consequently they have put a heavy stone on his tongue." She spilled a few drops of her drink in a toast. "To your ancestors," she said.

"Thank you, Linda,"—Kojo spilled a few drops of his drink and Deanie spilled a few drops of hers—"and thank you, Deanie." He took a drink.

"The stone is lifted," Linda said, smiling, her cheeks glistening.

"Yes," Kojo said. "Now if we could only lift the stone from someone else's tongue." He paused and began sliding his keys in a circle around his glass. "We would be in much better shape."

"Susan's?" Deanie asked.

"Of course," Kojo said. "You're very perceptive—which is one reason I like you." His mood was lightening up. Linda raised her eyebrows. "And to you," he said to Linda, chuckling, "sometimes silences, well placed, are signs of perceptions—as in good music." He toasted the two of them. "But silences poorly placed make for bad music." He got up and took some ice cubes from the freezer compartment. "And when the music gets bad, people stop dancing. The system begins to weaken and we have a problem." Kojo dropped the ice cubes into his drink.

"So what are you getting at?" Linda asked.

"Susan happens to have an old notebook of mine that might cause a great deal of trouble if it fell into the wrong hands. And she won't return it."

"Won't?" Deanie said.

"It's what you've been asking me about, that *thing* she has. I have to have it back. I've asked her a hundred times in a hundred different ways."

"What's in it?" Linda asked.

"As I said, it's an old notebook. With dated entries—which is part of the problem. At any rate, I have all kinds of stuff in it—lists for the greengrocer in London, phone numbers there and here, notes for my résumé, a couple of unfinished letters, calculations I'd made to determine miles per gallon on an old Dodge convertible that I was thinking of buying." He paused a moment and rubbed his forehead. "So among all of this are two lists of about eight or ten names each. One is titled 'Good Guys' and one is titled 'Bad Guys.'" He took a drink. "And it so happens that the 'Bad Guys' all hold positions in the government at home, and two of the 'Good Guys' were killed in an alleged coup attempt in May."

"And the date shows that the lists were written *before* the coup attempt?" Deanie asked. His eyes narrowed. "I mean the *alleged* coup attempt."

"Right." He looked at Linda. "Before you ask why I would do such a thing, let me tell you what happened. Near the end of April I was sitting there writing a few notes on how things looked at home." He gestured towards the sofa. "Just before this—the same evening—I had been having a rambling chat with Carl Peterson. He'd been talking about the bombing in Vietnam and then he went on in general about getting priorities straight. He started with the President and worked his way down through the governor's office to the vice-president's office here at Peeze, threw in some department heads, and then he jumped to Ghana. And as he always does, he got into a whole thing about good guys and bad guys. And then, after he left, I sat there a while with the notebook and made the lists."

"And one night after Susan gave you a ride home from your night class your mind was on *other* things, and you left the notebook in her car," Linda said, leaning back against the counter and looking away with a sigh as if she'd had the last word on the subject.

Kojo looked at her for a few seconds without speaking. "No. She stopped by here one day—it was still April, before Nkrumah died—to use the telephone. She had to call the mechanic to see if Barett's station wagon was ready in order to find out if she would have to stay around to give Barett and Deanie a ride home in her car. She grabbed the notebook to write down a phone number or something. She had Gary with her. And when she left she took the notebook with her, and I didn't notice it, and I don't think she did either."

"But she didn't waste any time in reading it," Linda said.

"I don't know. And I don't care. I didn't miss the damn thing for over a week. I just want it back."

"What does she want in exchange?" Deanie said.

"I don't know. Perhaps she imagines that I'm involved in something exciting that she could be a part of. I know she likes applause—the feeling of getting it—"

"We all do," Linda said.

"That's right," Kojo said, "and she has a very strong need to accomplish things on her own, by herself."

"What do you think she wants?" Linda asked.

"I just don't know."

"Maybe she doesn't know either," Deanie said.

"I think you're right," Kojo said. "I've known her for five years, and I just can't put my finger on anything."

"But maybe you did," Linda said, raising her eyebrows, and winking at Deanie.

"That's enough," Kojo said. "I just have to get the notebook back. If the names in it get out, some people I know are going to shit blue flames."

141

NINE

As they approached the Shamrock Tavern the rain drops on the
windshield sparkled green in the light from the neon sign. Iris's
old cream-colored Ford was parked under one of the two bay
windows that bulged out on either side of the front door. Zerk
pulled into the bumpy dark parking lot alongside the old white-
clapboard building, and Deanie saw the only other vehicle there
was a green pickup parked under the last of the four windows
that ran along the side of the tavern. Deanie thought the truck
looked like the one driven by the carpenter who was working on
the gatehouse.

Zerk parked by the first window. "I wonder if the kitchen's
open?" he said. "I could sure use a sandwich."

"Don't worry, Iris will make you one," she said.

Iris was sitting on a stool on her side of the L-shaped bar,
talking with the carpenter who sat across from her a third of the
way down the bar that came out from Deanie's left and then
turned to stretch away from her on the left side of the low-
ceilinged room. Iris looked good in the beige pullover. The

wings of the black and yellow butterfly embroidered on the front seemed to reach up from her shoulders and flutter towards her long gold earrings.

Deanie brushed rain drops from her cheeks as Zerk came in behind her. "The Queen of the Silver Dollar," she said, greeting Iris with a phrase from a song she'd heard on the juke box.

"More like the queen of the plug nickel tonight," Iris said.

"Where is everybody?" Zerk asked. He sat by the wall on one of the two stools on the near end of the bar, his back to the bay window.

"Sunday nights are usually quiet," Iris said. There were some fellas in earlier, but they left around seven to go see a new topless dancer out at the Wigwam." She put her hand on the carpenter's wrist. "But Jacob stayed to keep me company. Do you know Jacob the carpenter?"

"Yes," Deanie said, smiling. She sat on the stool on Zerk's right. "And, Jacob, do you know Zerk? He lives in the stable apartment up the drive from my place."

The carpenter nodded and slid his change across the bar towards Iris. "Dare first ones are on me," he said in his Swedish accent.

"Thank you," Deanie said. Zerk nodded and lifted his hand in acknowledgement. Jacob's clear hazel eyes sparkled and his ruddy cheeks glowed.

"Two drafts?" Iris asked.

They nodded.

"Please," Zerk said.

Beyond the carpenter, past the end of the bar, the poolroom in back, with its three-quarter-sized coin-operated table, was dark. Johnny Cash was singing about a burning ring of fire on the jukebox on the far wall of the barroom. On the wall to the right of the jukebox hung a homemade game board of painted numbers and cup hooks towards which the players threw little rubber vacuum cleaner belts. Back to her right, in front of the other bay window, by the cigarette machine, a strip of black electrical tape on the large maroon and gray floor tiles marked the throwing line. The wall opposite the bar was taken up by four booths upholstered in red vinyl—a large round one in the far corner by the game board, and three rectangular ones along the wall, each with a black-topped table. The four windows, half-covered by red and white checkered curtains, brightened the dark wood paneling and reflected the dim lights on the shelves behind Iris.

Iris set paper coasters and draft beers in front of Deanie and Zerk, picked a dollar from Jacob's money, and rang up the sale. Deanie smiled at Jacob and lifted her beer.

"Healt," he said.

"And health to you," Deanie said. He smiled and looked really cheerful in his starched white shirt and the yellow lumber company cap tipped way back on his head. Deanie noticed that he apparently had taken off a red necktie and stuck it into his shirt pocket. A few inches of the tie hung out of his pocket like a tongue. Above it she saw drawn on his shirt two red eyes with black eyelashes and a black nose.

"You like my doggie?" Jacob said.

"That's very clever," Deanie said. It looked like lipstick and eye liner, something Iris would do if she had a chance, and when she looked at Iris her broad smile told her that she was right. "What'll your wife say, Jacob?"

He looked down at the drawing and reached up to pull the bill of his cap down a couple of inches. "Oh...she might yump up and down a little." His face reddened. "Maybe I'm skating on tin ice." He got off the squeaky stool, picked up his change, put a dollar back, and turned for the door. "I tink I'm on tin ice. And today is August tirteent—not a lucky number. Good night." He waved to Iris as if he was wiping a huge pane of glass.

"Safe home," she said.

Jacob pulled his cap down a little more and went out.

"You ought to be ashamed of yourself," Deanie said, half seriously.

"No harm done," Iris said. "He was havin' a good time." She wiped the bar and stuck the dollar into her tip glass by the cash register.

"I see you have your car tonight," Deanie said.

"Yeah. After all the work we did on my bike yesterday, my tranny still ain't workin' right. It's so depressing."

"Can't you pick up a rebuilt transmission?" Zerk asked.

Iris brushed her hair back from her cheek and turned on her stool. Her black denim skirt emphasized the paleness of her long thighs. "I'd like to, but it's a really old Italian bike, and I just can't find parts for it."

"What kind is it?" Zerk asked.

"It's a Laverda, a two-fifty. I bought it last spring from a guy who used to come in here. He was a union steward out at the nuclear plant."

"Maybe Deanie could send the parts to you from Italy."

"I could try," Deanie said.

"Hey—that's right. You're goin' to Italy pretty soon."

Iris's face lit up. "I'll draw you some pictures of the parts I need and you can just show 'em to the guy at the"—she paused—"parts counter." She slapped the bar in front of Zerk and leaned towards him with a huge open-mouthed smile. "You been around the world. They must have motorcycle parts places in Italy. Right?"

"I'm sure they do," he said.

"That's super." She got up and drew herself a beer.

"Could I have some quarters for the pool table while you're up?" Zerk got off his stool and put two dollars on the bar. "I think I'll go back and sharpen up my triple-bank shot."

"Hot stuff," Deanie said.

"We'll see," he said, knitting his brow, and picking up the quarters and his beer. The old floor under the vinyl tiles creaked as he moved away.

Deanie knew that Zerk was going back to the pool table to let them talk in private. He stopped by the quiet juke box, looked over the selections, and went into the back room and pulled the light chain that hung over the table. He punched in the quarters freeing the stored balls to rumble down the trough at the side.

Iris went to the air conditioner that rested on the sill of the painted-over window by the other end of the bar and turned it down a couple of notches. "Is that okay?"

"That's fine," Deanie said.

"Sometimes the humming vibrates the glasses on the shelves and everything buzzes." She shook her hands in front of her and made a cross-eyed, crazy face. "That's a pretty shirt. You look good in light blue."

"That's what I told my mother when she asked me why I wore jeans all the time," Deanie said. "I said I looked good in light blue."

"I heard the same thing. Believe me. And, 'How come you're not wearin' a bra?'"

"Right. I've heard that more than once."

"My mother used to tell me that I looked like one of my father's aunts, a big Russian peasant woman." Iris held her arms out and touched her fingertips in front of her. "Big Russian woman," she said. She tucked in her chin to widen her face. "Nes-ter-vich. Even sounds fat." She straightened up and brushed her hair back from her face. "It also sounds a little like 'nasty bitch,' which some of the dim-bulbs used to call me in high school." She sat on the stool. "'Deanie Hollins'—that sounds pretty harmless. How'd you make out with that?"

"Okay," Deanie said. "An occasional 'Deanie-weenie,' but that's all."

"You were lucky." Iris leaned over towards her, lifted her hair away from the bowls of olives and maraschino cherries, and glanced towards the door and the back room. "'Nasty bitch' is only half of it"—she lowered her voice—"I've had to live with 'Iris the virus.'" She leaned back and looked genuinely depressed.

"That's tough."

Iris sighed and sat up a little. "Yeah. My mom said 'Iris' meant 'rainbow'—all pretty and sparkly."

"You *are* pretty and sparkly," Deanie said.

She smiled. "Thanks." She brushed her cheek with her fingertips, and, as her smile faded, she looked Deanie in the eye for a moment. "And thanks for coming by."

"I'm glad Zerk could give me a ride." She turned to see him reaching around the green felt, setting up the balls for practice, his yellow and white polo shirt tight over his shoulder muscles. "Just one thing," Deanie said. She paused and Iris leaned over attentively. "Could you make Zerk a sandwich? He doesn't want to interrupt us."

"Sure." Iris walked to the end of the bar, lifted the hinged section of the top, and went back to take Zerk's order. Deanie watched him setting up the balls, checking the cues for straightness.

Iris came out of the small kitchen that was off the poolroom, set Zerk's sandwich on a table, and brought a plate of cheese and crackers back to the bar.

Deanie took a piece of cheese. "Maybe one bite," she said, as she popped it into her mouth. "It all adds up."

"Yeah, it does." Iris pinched at the sides of her pullover. "You've still got that modeling job, haven't you?"

Deanie nodded.

"Do you like it?"

"It's a job. The first day was a little strange, but since then it's been tolerable."

"Are you going to keep doing it when you come back from Italy?"

"I doubt it. It's something that pays well, and I just sort of fell into it."

"But you got the looks, don't kid yourself."

"Well..."

"My body ain't bad, I don't think," Iris said, "but my nose would go right off the page, and they'd have to snip all of my

147

pictures." She stuck out two fingers and opened and closed them in front of her face like a scissors.

"I don't think so," Deanie said.

"So you and Barett don't think my nose is too big. That's nice, but not enough to get me a modeling job." Iris plunged Jacob's glass into the sudsy wash tank, the rinse tank, and set it on the drain rack. "This pays okay too, especially with tips, you know, but I really want to teach full time and maybe just tend bar in the summer."

"You're subbing now, aren't you?"

"Oh yeah. Well, actually not until they call me in September. I'm on the list, but they have to call me." Iris dumped her beer, dropped a handful of ice into a rocks glass, and filled it with white wine.

"Is there any reason they wouldn't?"

"It's hard to say. I had a little problem at a high school last spring, and I'll just have to wait and see."

"What happened?"

"It was really stupid, and embarrassing. And I don't embarrass easily. I mean sometimes I'm the only woman in here, and I'm waiting on thirty hard hats and a bunch of wise guys from the university, you know. I do just fine. Anyhow," she said, "I was coverin' the study hall, and I had on a skirt that wasn't really that short, but it was a wrap-around, and it happened to get twisted around and come open in back—way open—so I was walkin' around the study hall for twenty minutes with my ass hanging out." She shook her head and sighed. "And I thought it was my nose. I saw everybody lookin' at me, and lookin' at each other, and giggling into their hands, you know, and I thought it was my nose. I kept rubbin' my nose till it hurt."

"Nobody told you?"

"Not until the bell. This dumpy lookin' girl with acne stopped and told me on her way out. I could've died." She took a sip of her wine. "At least I didn't have any holes in my underwear."

Deanie shook her head. "That's terrible." She finished her beer and Iris took her glass and filled it. "So what happened?"

"Needless to say, the principal called me into his office. And, get this, he said he understood there'd been some problem in my study hall, and he didn't want to discuss it. He said it would be hard for me to sub there for a while. He said there'd have to be a cooling-off period. And then he said, he said, 'Maybe if you wore a skirt more often you'd be able to manage some of the peculiarities of fashion design.' Can you believe that?"

Deanie nodded. "He wasn't even talking to you."

"You're right. He was talkin' to a student or his daughter or somethin'. What an asshole."

"You must have felt terrible after all of that."

"I did, but it kinda worked out. I came in here to see what was goin' on, and I ran into Barett and Zerk and they asked me to play pool with 'em. Then later on they took me out for dinner at the Elk Hotel." Iris sat on the stool and began examining the hem of her skirt. She rolled up the edge, pinched out the wrinkles, and then smoothed it across her thighs. "And then a week later Barett stopped by and asked me out for dinner, and I went." She picked up her glass and put a coaster under it. "So what did you want to see me about?"

Deanie laughed. "That's not the way I remember it."

Iris looked up in mock bewilderment. "Oh." She paused. "Yeah—I guess you're right. I wanted to see you." She smoothed her hem again and rubbed the back of her neck. "I don't know what Susan's told you. I see Barett once in a while. But I ain't bendin' his arm. His ole lady ain't no peach. I mean, you know, she's been foolin' around with Kojo and, you know, Barett's a really sensitive guy. What's good for the goose is good for the gander."

Deanie picked a maraschino cherry out of the bowl, twirled it in front of her and set it back. "How do you know—I'm sorry, I mean how does Barett know that Susan's fooling around with Kojo?"

"Don't worry. He knows. She's been growing away from him, and people tell him things, you know."

"So he's convinced."

"He knows. Believe me."

"I can't see them," she paused, "I can't see Kojo and Susan getting involved with each other," Deanie said. She realized that there wasn't much else she could say to Iris. If she said "because she's married" or "because he wants to avoid entanglements" or "because she's too smart" it would sound like she was putting Iris down. And, after all, she came to listen to her.

"They've been close for a long time, before Kojo even came here," Iris said.

"That's true. They may even have been lovers in London, and that would account for"—she sat up straight, flipped her hair over her shoulders, and extended her arm in a theatrical gesture—"knowing glances and half-formed smiles across the crowded room."

"What if it was a crowded bedroom?"

Deanie looked down the bar and watched the cue ball going cushion-to-cushion in the cone of light and back to Zerk. A ball fell through a pocket with a clunk. "Nice shot," she said loudly.

Zerk stood back from the light, chalking his cue. "This is for you." He bent over and shot. The cue ball went around the table through the colored balls like a comet curving through a solar system. Something clicked and a ball dropped into the corner pocket. Zerk stood back from the cone of light and twisted the tip of his cue in the chalk and slowly nodded towards her. She felt something. She wanted him.

"Did you say what I think you said?" Deanie said.

"Maybe not a *crowded* bedroom," Iris said.

"And Barett's certain?" she said, looking back at Iris.

"People have seen 'em together at Kojo's place. Lots of times."

"That's hard to believe." She looked back at Zerk. He was squatting by the pool table, his arm resting on the edge, reaching out to position a ball with his forefinger. The way his muscles

150

worked made the visible part of his body look like the top half of a Renaissance sculpture that she'd seen in a picture somewhere.

"Looks like we've got some company." Iris was looking towards the parking lot. Deanie saw headlights pull up to a window and shut off. They watched the heavy wooden door swing out. It was Kojo. He leaned into the doorway and glanced back over his shoulder as if he was being pursued and came in.

"Greetings," he said. He stood there, feet apart, head up, looking around the room.

"Hello, Kojo," Deanie said.

"Hi," Iris said. She put a coaster on the bar across the corner from Deanie. Kojo glanced around the room, looked back towards Zerk, and sat on the stool. He had rolled up the sleeves of his white, short-sleeved shirt, and Deanie could smell a hint of curry and sweet wine about him.

"This one's on me," Zerk said, tapping the coaster. He was standing by Kojo, sliding his glass towards Iris.

"Thank you, Zerk," Kojo said. He raised his eyebrows and nodded vigorously towards Iris. "A Scotch on the rocks, please."

Zerk took his draft, put the money down, and came back around Kojo to his stool on Deanie's left. "So what brings you out on a night like this?"

"It's not so bad—it's stopped raining. I was just coming from a B.S.A. meeting, and I thought I recognized your car." Iris set his drink on the coaster. "I salute you from afar," he said, toasting Zerk.

Zerk nodded and took a drink. "Just curious—" he said, "what does 'B.S.A' stand for?"

"Black Students' Association," Kojo said. "They had a meeting at a member's apartment with a guest speaker who's just back from visiting a few countries in Africa."

"Was it a good meeting?" Deanie asked.

"I think so," Kojo said. "The students are beginning to learn that it's going to take more than a few scholarships here, and a few black studies courses there to make a difference in the way things are."

Deanie realized that her talk with Iris was over—at least for now. And in any case it had come down to Iris more or less saying that she believed Barett because she wanted to. And Deanie knew that for her own part she wanted to believe that Susan and Kojo were not having an affair. She guessed by the look on Iris's face that she also was acknowledging the end of their conversation. "I hope things work out," Deanie said.

"What!" Kojo said. "You *hope* things *work out*?" His jaw dropped in dismay. "You *know* what the racist monster is doing; you can hear its tail smashing people's bones around the world; you can see its claw marks on your neighbors' faces; you can smell its rotten breath in your—"

"I was talking to *Iris*," she said, waving her hand in front of his face. "We were talking before you came in."

Kojo stretched his eyebrows way up, nodded at her and Iris, and took a drink. "I'm glad. That's good. I couldn't believe that you would have responded to a glimpse of the monster in such a light-hearted way."

"Did something happen after your meeting?" Deanie asked.

"What do you mean?"

"I think," Zerk said, leaning closer, "that in spite of the immensity and intensity of the subject of your meeting, she was a little surprised by your reaction to what she said."

"Umm." Kojo's eyebrows went way up again, and he nodded at Zerk and Deanie.

"I can speak for myself," Deanie said.

"She can—I know," Kojo said. His face softened and, laughing gently, he glanced from her to Zerk to Iris and back to her.

"Sorry," Zerk said.

"That's all right," Deanie said. "Not to worry." She winked at Kojo.

Kojo looked at Iris and pointed to their glasses. "Two more," he said.

"I've never heard you say much about Africa," Zerk said.

"Liberation for our brothers"—he touched Deanie's arm—
"and sisters has always been right up there." Kojo extended his
arm towards the ceiling as if indicating the top of a list. "But
there are immediate concerns in West Africa, in Ghana, that have
to be addressed." He moved his hand back and forth as if to
indicate many items on the top of a list.

Iris took the empty beer glasses and set fresh drafts on the
coasters.

"What about somebody like Henry Trainer?" Deanie asked.

"What about him?" Kojo said.

"Well..." She glanced at Zerk. "He was at the West End."

"I remember you telling me," Zerk said, nodding.

She looked back at Kojo. "What about his role?"

"I don't know him, and I can't speak for him," Kojo said.
"He's an American, after all, and so are you. I understand what
he's saying about the hellish conditions of your cities. One of
our problems at home is the tremendous movement of people to
the cities. I know what he's talking about, but I also know that
the dropping price of our cocoa on the world market causes
tremendous problems for us." Kojo moved his glass in a little
circle on the bar. "But as for Henry Trainer, his general
direction may be all right in some ways, but in a sense he
reminds me of the chap who drowned in the dive for life—a little
too wide to get through some of the tight spots in life."

"Guess what?" Iris said. She was leaning on the bar, looking
past Kojo. "It looks like the fellas are back from the Wigwam."

Deanie saw headlights and amber truck lights moving in the
lot. There were still lights moving in the lot when the door
opened and Susan Burkhart came in.

"Is Barett here?" she asked.

Iris slouched on her stool as though she was trying to keep
out of sight, rolled her eyes, and straightened up. "He hasn't
been in today."

"You all look so cozy. I never imagined..." Susan's voice
trailed off and she rested her hand on the cigarette machine, her

153

pink boatnecked top and yellow shorts bright against her dark tan. She looked to Deanie as if she was in a trance or incredibly stoned. She turned to walk along the booths, touching the top of each seat as if to verify its existence. Nobody said anything. They were all watching her. She stopped by the game board, examined a vacuum cleaner belt, and put it back on a hook. "Vacuum cleaner belts." She clasped her hands under her chin. "Does Barett play with vacuum cleaner belts?" She looked towards the ceiling. "I should think he'd play with garter belts."

Kojo pulled out a stool. "Come. Sit down. Sit with us."

Susan smiled, brushed her hair back from her face, and, patting her shoulder, her smile faded. "My bag. I left my bag in the car," she said. "How forgetful of me."

"Not to worry," Kojo said. "Come. Sit."

"Those guys won't take your bag," Iris said, looking towards the windows. Deanie could see that Susan was avoiding eye contact with Iris. "I wonder what they're doin' out there?"

"Susan," Deanie said, "has it stopped raining?" She wanted to engage her in some simple talk.

"Yes. A while ago. Though it may be raining in Spain...in the plain...or on the plain, if it's a Stearman Trainer."

Deanie brought both elbows up to the bar and folded her arms on the edge. On the plane. She hadn't heard of a Stearman Trainer since her first day at Randall's place. She began to wonder if Susan was all right, and for a moment she wondered if she herself was okay. Susan's mentioning the Stearman Trainer had made her feel a twinge of discomfort. She glanced at Zerk. He was building a little log cabin on the bar with toothpicks. For an instant she wished they could both shrink and go into the little cabin and close the door and cuddle. Zerk looked up.

"Your tan really looks good, Susan," Zerk said.

"Thank you." She sighed and climbed onto the stool.

Iris put a coaster in front of her. "What would you like?" She seemed to be looking past Susan. Deanie saw there were still lights in the lot, but they had stopped moving. A pair of headlights went out.

"I'll have a beer and a ball," Susan said.

"What?" Iris looked startled.

"A beer and a ball. Zerk says that's what all the hard hats drink. I've decided to start wearing a hard hat." Susan poked at her hair with her fingers and tipped her head as if she was looking at herself in the mirror behind Iris.

Iris rolled her eyes, set a shot glass in front of Susan, and reached for the bar whiskey. "Is this okay?"

"Is that what the hard hats drink?"

"Some of them."

"Then that's fine."

Susan still hadn't made eye contact with Iris. Deanie couldn't figure out what had come over her. She knew from sitting with Gary that drugs weren't a part of Susan's life. She sounded drunk, but her physical movements seemed so measured, so precise, that she couldn't be drunk. It seemed almost as if part of Susan was drunk and part of her wasn't. Suddenly Deanie wondered where Gary was. "Where's Gary?"

"Where's Gary?" Susan looked puzzled. "Gary's in bed."

"Do you want me to go and keep an eye on him while you and Kojo talk?"

Susan looked directly at Iris for the first time and seemed to be thinking over an answer. "Do you have any cigarillos?"

Iris turned back to the counter and the shelves and moved the blue and red display cards of lighter flints, rabbit's foot key chains, and packaged handkerchiefs; she looked behind the cerebral palsy canister, the PBA canister, the beer nut rack, and the gallon jug of pickled sausages; she opened a couple of drawers below the counter, peered into them, and turned to Susan. "How about some Red Man?" Iris made a crazy face at Deanie, shrugged, and leaned back, shutting the drawers with her rear end.

Kojo had put on his shades and seemed to be studying Susan.

Susan looked at Deanie. "Am I supposed to talk to Kojo about something?"

Deanie wanted to say something about the notebook, but she'd only heard one side of the story. She looked over through the windows, trying to formulate an answer. More headlights had gone out. "I just thought—"

Kojo leaned close to Deanie. "Susan's not feeling well," he whispered.

"What's 'Red Man'?" Susan asked.

"Chewing tobacco," Iris said.

Susan ran her fingers through her hair and shook her head.

"Would you do that, Deanie?" Susan said.

"Go watch Gary?"

"Please. Unless Barett's there. He may be there. He went out at five to shoot a game of pool. And then he and I were going to go to a movie. Or maybe we weren't going to go to a movie. I just don't know anymore."

Deanie looked at Zerk. "Okay?" Zerk nodded and got off his stool. Iris was standing, leaning back against the counter by the cash register, her arms folded in front of her. Kojo's face was serious, his lips slightly pursed as though he was straining to hear or see something miles away. Deanie stood up. "Thanks, Iris."

Iris came to the end of the bar and leaned over to Deanie and Zerk. "Is she flipped out, or what?"

"It seems like part of her is," Deanie said.

"It's the uninvolved part of her," Zerk said. "The uninvolved part of her is off on a bender."

Iris leaned closer and frowned, her hair falling away from her shoulders to sweep the bar. "I don't think she's been drinkin'."

"I know," Zerk said.

"And she hasn't touched her drinks here," Deanie said.

"I know," Zerk said.

Iris nodded as though she understood, and Deanie slid her hand out and rested her fingers on Iris's hand. "Good luck."

"Thanks for coming." Iris leaned back and picked up their glasses, the bar rag in her hand bumping over the toothpicks.

"There goes our cabin," Deanie said.

"What?" Zerk asked.

Deanie pointed at the toothpicks spread on the bar. "Wasn't that a log cabin?"

Zerk shrugged. "Sort of, I guess."

Suddenly Deanie was taken up with the sounds of loud voices and shuffling shoes in front of the bay window on the other side of the door. There were thumps against the door as if someone was trying to push it open, some shouts, and somebody pulled the door open and they all came in.

There was the blond, forty-year-old, former Golden Gloves star from Michigan, tall, toothless, and reeling; the pimple-faced kid from the Chevron station, bug-eyed and laughing; a black guy with a flat-top haircut who was known for playing Neil Diamond's "Sweet Caroline" on the juke box at closing time; two dark-haired guys in jackets with trade union emblems; a handsome man with styled white hair; the administrative assistant from the Anthropology department at Peeze; the redhead who cut grass and drove snow plows for the town. There were hands waving and shoes stomping and more guys and smells of motor oil and whiskey and shaving lotion. Some of them were carrying in two two-by-fours, side by side, with a wood panel lashed on top, and Deanie saw the gold spike heels; the bare legs, the lashed-on chair; the gold-feathered G-string; the tassled nipple covers; and the live boa constrictor draped around the woman's shoulders. She was smiling, and her eyes were wide. Holding up the other end of the litter came Barett Burkhart and one of his drinking buddies, smiling from ear to ear, smiling one stretched-out smile from Barett's right ear all the way across to his buddy's left ear. Seeing the four of them at the bar, Barett and his buddy froze, and the smile rolled up under their mustaches like a snapped window shade.

Deanie imagined why Barett looked startled—he had missed his date with Susan and—worse—he saw that they all had been having a conversation without the benefit of his guidance. It was harder to guess why his friend looked so startled—either he felt uncomfortable being seen with Barett, or something about all of them being there bothered him. Was it Iris and Susan's being together? She wondered. What could they say to each other that would affect him? She watched the woman adjust the snake on her shoulders. Funny, she thought, how their parading around with the nearly naked woman seemed almost irrelevant to her wondering why they looked startled.

The ex-boxer was holding his hand up over the crowd. He backed against the juke box. "Quiet!" he shouted. "Shut up a minute!" He jumped and tapped his fist on the ceiling, and they quieted down. The gas station attendant kept laughing and the big blond clamped his huge hands around the kid's head as if it were a melon he was about to pull from a vine. "Since you couldn't come up to the Wigwam with us," he said to Iris, "we asked Shareena, here, if she'd do us the honor of accompanying us back here to brighten up your evening. And and as you can see we've got the queen of the jungle—" he stopped talking and seemed to be staring at Kojo as though seeing him there had made him stop to reconsider the line he was giving Iris.

Susan turned back to Deanie and Zerk. "Can I go with you?"

"Sure," Zerk said. "But why don't you just let Deanie drive you in your car if you don't feel like driving?"

"Of course," Susan said. "Why didn't I think of that?"

"I'm going too," Kojo said. He got up with Susan and raised his hand towards the ex-boxer. "Don't let us stop you."

"As I was saying..." the ex-boxer said.

Deanie followed Zerk to the door, and Susan and Kojo came up next to her. Barett and his friend were by the door, holding onto their ends of the two-by-fours, Barett in a tan work shirt, and his friend in a black T-shirt. Kojo looked back at the dancer. Deanie saw her looking at him. The dancer's eyes rested on puffy-looking cheeks that each bore a cluster of tiny pock marks. Her hair was waved and long, probably a wig, and held back by a gold headband. She ran her tongue sensually across her upper lip and lifted her hand to stroke the boa constrictor's jaw. "Nobody's twisting her arm," Kojo said.

"But maybe somebody's twisting Susan's," Barett said, leaning towards Kojo.

Susan stuck her arms out, straight at Barett's face, her palms down, her fingers spread, and, not saying a word, she slowly rolled her hands palms-up, palms-down, and palms-up. "Nobody's twisting my arm," she said.

Barett sighed, brought his hand up to pull at his beard, and let his corner of the litter down a couple of inches. "Well—"

"Watch it," his buddy said.

Barett dropped his hand and brought up the two-by-four. He bit at the corner of his mustache and squinted at Susan and Kojo. Some of the guys were sliding out stools at the bar, and the gas station attendant was massaging his ears. Iris was busy. Deanie saw that Barett had stopped squinting. The muscles around his eyes were relaxing. "I"—he lifted his hand for an instant and slapped it back under the two-by-four—"guess you're right." It looked like Barett had understood that there was—or had been— something between Susan and Kojo, something that was beyond his control, and maybe even beyond his comprehension.

Now Zerk was outside on the top step, holding the door open. Deanie went out. A car roared past with a broken muffler dragging a streak of sparks down the road.

"See you at home?" Susan said. Barett nodded. Deanie caught the door.

"Not to worry," Kojo said. He reached out and clasped Barett's shoulder. "Not to worry."

Barett's eyes narrowed to a fixed stare and he nodded rapidly, almost spastically, several times. The hard hats and the others who had returned from the Wigwam began moving towards the back room, and Barett inclined with them.

Kojo looked back at the dancer, and Susan brushed her hair from her face and they all came out.

Deanie followed Zerk to his car. She still wanted him. "Are you going back to your place?"

159

"Of course." He stood there rolling down his window.

"Can I come over?"

"I'll be waiting."

Kojo said good night and Deanie walked to Susan's car and waited for her. Through the tavern window she saw nearly everyone had crowded into the back room. Iris was sitting on her stool behind the bar, looking towards the back room, twisting a swizzle stick between her teeth. Just over the top of the crowd the dancer's head and shoulders appeared. She must be on the pool table, she thought. Suddenly the gas station attendant spun away from the crowd, wearing the feathered G-string over his head. Iris threw the bar rag at him, and the white-haired man came over and closed the curtains on the windows facing the parking lot.

TEN

Susan slept all the way home, and as Deanie woke her she was groggy and disoriented, as if she had a hangover. After a few minutes she got out of the car. "Thanks," Susan said, "I'll be okay."

Deanie walked to the steps with her, breathing deeply of the fresh air rippling in from the sound, wishing the dark leaves twisting against the stars would shake loose something from Susan about Kojo, the notebook. "You're sure you're going to be okay?" Susan nodded. "I'm glad you're feeling better"— Deanie folded her arms and rocked her foot on the corner of the step—"and maybe this isn't the best time to ask, but I was wondering if, as long as you trust me with Gary and you trust me with your car, if you'd trust me with something else?"

Susan looked puzzled. "What?"

Deanie stuck her hands into her back pockets. "What's the story with Kojo's notebook?"

161

Susan bit at the inside of her lip. Deanie pivoted her heel on the brick walk and brushed the frayed toe of her sneaker across the grass.

"I've got the notebook," Susan said. "You probably knew that. I got it by accident. It's in my safe deposit box in the city. I'm going to give it back to Kojo. It's just that he's made such a big deal of it." Susan rubbed her hands on her shorts and haltingly dug her fingers into her thighs, and her lower lip began to tremble. "I'm going to give it back to him." Deanie saw what she wanted, what she needed, and she put her arms around her as Susan's hands came up and pulled her close. "Hold me," Susan said, "please hold me. Nobody holds me anymore." Deanie held her and looked across the edge of the mansion's roof at the stars. "I guess I was using the notebook to hold Kojo," Susan whispered. "I was using it to hold him."

"But you've known Kojo for a long time. You didn't need the notebook to have him close to you."

"I did after I married Barett. After we were married our friendship changed—and it shouldn't have."

"Do you mean you and Kojo aren't lovers?"

Susan dropped her head, and Deanie felt her tremble, felt Susan's heart beating against hers. "No, we're not," she said, holding her tight, "and Barett and I aren't either. Not any more." A long moment passed, and Susan sighed deeply, dropped her arms, and turning away, went up the steps.

* * *

It was almost eleven o'clock as Deanie drove Zerk's car onto the campus. After she'd left Susan she'd gone back to her place, showered, and tried to read, but what Susan had said and the way she had felt, trembling in her arms, had left Deanie so upset that she felt compelled to see Kojo and talk to him about Susan. A couple walking in the middle of the road moved off to give her room to pass. Now that the summer session had ended the place was nearly deserted. Some people were sitting on the fenders of two cars parked by the lit-up tennis courts, there were a few cars in the infirmary lot, a Volkswagen bus and an old Toyota in the darkened Humanities lot, and a white Porsche and a new yellow Jaguar were parked by the side entrance to the physics building, where lights shone on the second and third floors. She parked under the street light in the angle-parking area for dorm visitors and walked towards Kojo's end of the building. Right across from the entrance, she saw Susan's car parked by the curb.

And there they were. She could see them through the bushes that reached across the window—Susan and Kojo standing in his living room. She could hear them through the open window. She wasn't a voyeur, and she wasn't an eavesdropper. But here she was, and she wasn't going to sit in the car until Susan left. She stepped closer to the window.

Kojo was wearing a short, red and white bathrobe, and Susan was still in her pink top and shorts. She felt wet pine needles on her forearm from the trees by the wall as she strained to see into the kitchen and beyond.

"This," Kojo was saying, "is not some child's notebook of fantasies. This...this...this is this!" He swept his open hand down to smack the end table, tipping a pewter vase onto the floor.

"A table? Yes, that's not a notebook," Susan said. "That's a table. You can't read a table...unless it's a table of contents or a ta—"

"Damnit, Susan. Please. Listen to me. You can't be queen of the continent." Susan shook her head as though she couldn't believe what he was saying. "She won't let you," Kojo said. "She is her own queen and always will be. And by 'continent' I also mean nation, city, town, village, compound, and household. You can't be queen of any of them." He put his hands on his head and walked to the kitchen table and back. "Why am I saying this?"

Susan sat on the arm of the chair. "Maybe you like to hear yourself talk."

163

He glared at her. "You—" he paused. "You shouldn't—" he paused again. "Say such things," he said.

She looked startled. "I'm sorry," she said, folding her arms. "I'm sorry for saying that."

His voice softened a bit. "Susan, for the hundredth time, do you want something in exchange for the notebook?" She moved her hands on her arms as though she was having a chill. He waited for an answer, but she didn't say anything. "Will you please give back the notebook?"

"What if I asked you to return all of our good times together?"

"I wouldn't want to," he said. He sat on the sofa. Deanie guessed that Susan was trying to bring up something, to express something, they'd shared in the past. Kojo rubbed his hands back over his head. "What are you getting at?"

"There's more to me than meets the eye."

"I know that, Susan. I've never said otherwise." He paused. "Just give me the bloody notebook."

"What if I can't find it?"

"What do you mean by that?" he said, his head tipping back, his eyes narrowing.

"What do I mean?" She got up and went to the door. "Do I mean *anything*?" Her eyebrows arched inquisitively and she turned her head slowly from side to side, her eyes now questioning, now pleading, her hand reaching for the doorknob. She opened the door, took a deep breath, and shook her head. "I'll bring it back from my safe deposit box at the end of the week. At least a bloody copy of it." She mimicked a burst of laughter and went out, and as far away as she was, Deanie realized with a start, that as Susan turned away, her face again trembled just as it had that day they had stopped at the gas station on their way home from the city, when Susan realized that the man caught in the closet at the party had been Barett.

Deanie watched Susan drive away. She went around to the patio door and knocked. The patio light came on, the drapes moved, Kojo peered out for a moment, and slid the door open.

"Come in. You just missed an interesting show."

"I saw part of it," she said, "I was coming up to the building just before the vase went flying." She saw the vase under the edge of the sofa, picked it up, and as she reached to set it back on the end table it slipped from her fingers and dropped to the floor. "Sorry," she said.

"Not to worry," Kojo said, picking up the vase. "It's unbreakable."

"Like your will?" Deanie said.

Kojo laughed and set the vase back on the table. "You're too much, Deanie," he said, stepping over to the bookshelf. He picked up a glass of white wine. "I'm glad you came by when you did," he said. "Did you hear Susan promise to return the notebook at the end of the week?" His eyebrows stretched way up, and he nodded vigorously.

"Yes, but what did she say about a copy?"

"She won't make any copies. That would put the whole thing in the realm of threats and blackmail—and that's not her thing at all. She wanted to be a part of something—some imaginative undertaking with a high purpose—and it's simply not there for her."

"That's the impression I got from Susan," she said. She figured Kojo was talking about some distant political event, though he could have been referring to Susan and Barett's marriage. "Mind if I sit down?"

Kojo turned to look through a stack of records. "Sit down," he said, "please. And fix yourself something to eat—there's some chicken in the refrigerator." Deanie looked into the refrigerator, poured herself a glass of water, dropped in a couple of ice cubes and a chunk of lemon, and sat at the small kitchen table. The music started on low volume and the saxophone was unmistakable as Kojo came around the partition with his glass of wine and sat by her.

"Sounds like Coltrane," she said.

Kojo nodded. "It's his *Blue Trane* album," he said, leaning towards her. "I think it's one of his best." He took a sip of his wine and leaned towards her. "So what's bugging you?"

"Nothing's bugging me," she said. "I'm just concerned about my friends."

"You seemed a little anxious when you arrived," Kojo said, "but now that Susan has decided to give back my notebook we should be celebrating." He took a drink of his wine. "At least I should be celebrating." He tapped his fingers on the table. "Of course, I don't have the notebook in hand." He rolled his hand over and opened and closed it. He looked at her and smiled. "The Kojo hand is patient," he said, "among other things." He took a sip of wine. "So," he said, pausing, "you've completed summer school work—with flying colors, I presume? And you'll be embarking on an adventure to Italy in two or three weeks..." Kojo lifted his hand and gestured to her as though to elicit a response.

"It's just been a long day," she said. Kojo slid down a little in his chair and clasped his hands over his stomach, the wide sleeves of the robe hanging away from his elbows. He nodded, waiting for her to continue. "I think talking to Susan before I came here started it," she said.

"Started it?"

"I don't know." Deanie ran her finger down the condensation on her glass. "You've never said much about knowing Susan before you came to Peeze." She took a sip of her ice water.

"Well, what do you want to know?"

"How you met her, what she was like..." Deanie pushed the ice cubes down into the water and watched them pop up.

"That's displacement," Kojo said, sitting up and resting his hands on the table.

"Displacement?" she said, wondering where his comment had come from.

166

"The ice cubes in the water," he said. "It just struck me in a funny way, seeing you push the ice cubes down like that." He glanced at his watch.

"Do you have to go someplace?" she said.

"Not at the moment," he said. He raised his eyebrows, smiled, took a sip of his wine, and seemed to relax a little more. "Once...upon...a...time..." he said slowly, and Deanie rested her elbows on the table, settled her chin into her hands, and listened. "I got a research position in London." He reached around the partition and brought out a black and gold book on African art. He put the book down between them and started turning the pages. "Susan was traveling a lot, and trying to decide what to do with her degree in economics. He stopped turning the pages and studied the picture of a sculpture of a mother nursing a child, looked across to a mask representing an elephant, and turned the page.

"I met Susan at a party the following summer. She came with some people who worked for a film company. She was visiting a young woman whom she had met at her university. Her friend had a flat in West Kensington that Susan subsequently kept for her when she went to Greece for a film project that lasted about six months.

"Susan was the first American woman that I ever spent any time with outside of university offices and such. She was twenty-two that summer." He paused. "What did she say? She said"—he paused—"she said in a letter, 'I was living high on ideas and you were living on high ideas, and when the two swirls of our mental lives crossed corners that night in London our highs filled the same mental spaces often enough to convince me that we were kindred spirits.'" Kojo pulled his hands from the book to his glass. "And I agreed.

"And this was in spite of the fact that Susan's family seemed to own much of the steel manufacturing in Pittsburgh, while my family had only the bare essentials for shelter and getting food." Kojo reached out and turned a page. Deanie saw a long-necked bird and a ceremonial headpiece.

"When I told Susan that my family had had the status of nobility for as long as anyone could remember, she told me how her great-grandfather had married a hard-working woman, and then how, as the years passed, whenever a really important steel-deal took place, one of their descendants had something to do with it." Kojo was looking at pictures of mythical beings with tusks, horns, and feathers.

"Susan and her younger sister Paula tried to show a certain amount of independence by being the first in the last two generations of their family not to go to an Ivy League university, but, as Susan acknowledged to me, it wasn't the kind of gesture that anyone was likely to notice." Kojo turned the pages past ceremonial bowls, men on horseback, initiation masks.

"Susan was vibrant. She could hold her own on the writhing dance floors of Soho, and she could talk constructively about problems in achieving African unity. The fact that she knew a lot about Nelson Mandela was surprising. And she knew such things as that, for example, it's probably not wise to expect Canadian wheat to thrive in a country in Africa just because it thrives in Canada.

"We saw each other fairly often until Susan went back to the States in the middle of December. I stayed in the flat in West Kensington and when she returned she had what amounted to a promise of a job here for me. After that Susan traveled a great deal, and I think she saw Arnold Moskey and Barett from time to time at fund-raising affairs for political candidates, or at poetry readings and that sort of thing in New York. I saw her once in the spring before I came here to start teaching." A page turned and now there was a little girl, and she was wrapped in the arms of a strong man on horseback, riding away towards the horizon. There were jeweled eyes beside the path and silver birds streaming overhead, and the strong man carried the little girl rhythmically, surely, rhythmically—'Wake up.' Little Susie, wake up.

"What?" Deanie said.

"You fell asleep," Kojo said.

She yawned and sat back in her chair. "Did you call me 'Little Susie?'"

"No." He laughed. "You must have been dreaming."

She shook her head. "I'm sorry I fell asleep," she said. "Did you say that you saw Susan once in the spring before you came here?"

"Yes, just before you nodded," Kojo said. "You didn't miss a thing."

Deanie got up and stretched. "I'm going to get going. Thanks for everything."

"I'll walk out to your car with you," he said.

Kojo opened the patio door and they went out. She felt a lot better than she had on the way over. She knew that didn't necessarily mean she could make Susan feel any better, but now at least she could remind her of some of the fine moments she had had with Kojo and that her past was far from empty. And then maybe it would be easier for her to give back the notebook and get on with—with what? she wondered. A few insects bumped around the light, and the dust on the concrete walk showed blotchy patterns where raindrops had fallen from the maple leaves as if the trees had been shedding tears for somebody. Kojo walked with his hands in the pockets of his bathrobe. Deanie had hooked her thumbs over the top of her jeans and, seeing Barett's station wagon sticking out on the other side of Zerk's car, she turned to Kojo to see if he had seen it.

"More company," Kojo said.

She could see Barett under the street light, sitting on his front fender, smoking a cigarette.

"Hello," Barett said. He flipped the cigarette butt into the street.

"Greetings, Barett," Kojo said.

"Hi, Barett," she said.

"Having a little night class?" Barett said, digging his fingers into his beard as if he was picking out burrs.

"No night classes," Kojo said. "It's time to relax."

Deanie figured Kojo was trying to size up Barett's mental state. "How did everything turn out at the Shamrock?" she asked.

"What about earlier?" Barett asked.

"What do you mean?" she asked.

"I was talking to Professor Dedu," Barett said.

"Earlier?" Kojo said.

"Didn't you and Susan have a night class a little while ago?"

"Susan stopped by just before Deanie got here," Kojo said. "Has something happened?"

"Has something *happened*?" Barett said. He dropped his hands to the fender and slid off. "Something's going to happen. It's time somebody in the city checks out you and your buddies from the U.N." Barett slid his hand along the fender and carefully stepped around to the front of the station wagon. "I'd like to know what you're trying to do to our marriage." He slowly lifted his hand from the hood and brought it to rest on his side, over his ribs. "Well?"

"I think you're on the wrong track," Kojo said.

"You think I'm on the wrong track?" Barett walked around to the other side of the station wagon and opened the door. "You'll find out what kind of a track I'm on. I'm going to keep right on my track—full steam." He put his hand on the edge of the roof and came around the door. "Deanie?" he said. She didn't answer. "Deanie?"

"What?"

"You're okay. I'm sorry you had to hear all of this."

She started to say "I'm sorry, too," but she just stood there and stared at him, and while he backed his station wagon away and got going she turned to Kojo. "Good night," she said.

"Good night, Deanie," he said, and he started back to his place.

Deanie got out her keys, and as Barett's station wagon disappeared into the darkness, she saw that he still hadn't turned on his lights.

ELEVEN

The next Saturday, as she sat yawning on the edge of her bed, Deanie saw the carpenter's helper in the yard picking up the scraps of wood and drywall that had piled up over the summer. Their work was nearly done, and as she watched him cleaning up the yard she realized that September was less than two weeks away. The noise of the debris banging into the bed of the pickup had waked her from a dream of being chased by a train and not being able to jump off the tracks. She stretched out her arms, straightened the sheet, and stood up. It must've been the sun on her face. The sun must have become the light on the engine. She wondered what had kept her from jumping off the tracks—debris from her own life?—and after a moment she yawned again. Sometimes she wished she could just take off on a magic carpet and go skimming across the treetops. She looked across the trees. Rising higher and higher, heading west, through the blue. She sighed. It was nearly one o'clock, and here it was— Zerk's thirtieth birthday. Everyone had given up trying to make the birthday party a surprise and now in a few minutes Zerk would be waiting for her to stop by on the way over to Iris's place. And for the hundredth time it seemed, she thought of Kojo and Susan, and all the bitter bullshit from Barett, and hoped that today Kojo would get back his notebook before anybody else got involved in the tug of war or whatever it was that was causing so much pain to her friends.

Deanie went through the living room to the tiny kitchen, put some water on to boil, and went around opening the drapes in the living room. She put on a Janis Joplin tape and took her tea into the bedroom where she stood at the low-silled window, watching Larry, the carpenter's helper, throwing scraps of wood and drywall into the old green truck. Now he seemed to notice her, and he turned away and looked back, turned away and looked back, and now he just stood there staring, and it dawned on her that the large men's T-shirt, the only thing she was wearing, was, from that second-floor angle, probably not covering her at all, and, as the boy's mouth fell open, she backed away from the window and sat on the edge of the bed. She sat there sipping her tea, wondering if he would be coming up with some excuse to see her—maybe to ask if he could use her telephone? She smiled, glanced in the mirror, and sipped her tea.

Going down the new stairway, Deanie breathed the scent of the unfinished pine, and on the porch she stopped to breathe deeply of the scents of cut grass and clover from the immense lawn that stretched across the estate. She stood there, holding the paper bag that held the leather headband she'd bought for Zerk, and looked around for the carpenter's helper. She saw him, standing on the other side of the truck, in the shade of the maple tree, one hand hooked around the back of his neck, the other holding a can of soda under his chin.

"Hello," she said.

"Hi." He dropped his hand from his neck.

"Are you going to the barbecue at Iris's?"

He nodded. "As soon as I haul this load away and get cleaned up." He finished the soda.

"You can use my shower if you want to," she said.

"Well"—he crushed the can and dropped it in with the trash—"I've gotta take my uncle's truck back and get my mom's car." He moved his head as though he had a muscle spasm in his neck.

"I'll see you at the barbecue," she said, smiling and pointing towards Iris's place.

"Okay." He waved, sat in the cab, closed the door, rattled it, it hadn't latched. He opened it way out, and slammed it.

Halfway between the gatehouse and Zerk's apartment Deanie heard the truck start, and as she looked back the carpenter's helper turned away as if he'd been caught staring, and the sagging truck creaked onto the dirt drive and rolled away towards the road, and for a moment she wondered if he had ever slept with a woman.

Zerk was leaning back on the trunk of his car, squinting in the sun, his heel resting on the bumper. Deanie straightened the collar on her sleeveless blouse and flipped her hair back over her shoulders. He slid his boot from the bumper and straightened up.

"Happy Birthday." She handed him the bag.

"Hey. Thanks." He stared at her, smiling, for a moment, and then took the headband out of the bag. "Wow. Leather. This is great." He took her in his arms and she met his kiss and felt his tongue all around hers and now she turned her head and rested her cheek on his upper arm.

"Let's go to the party," she said.

"If you say so." Zerk nodded and started walking, fastening the headband in place. "This is really great," he said, "just what I needed."

"I thought so," she said. "It's supposed to keep your head from swelling." She snatched the bag from his hand and stuffed it into her pocket.

"Come on," he said, "it's my birthday. Gimme a break."

As they approached the mansion Zerk picked an apple from a branch hanging by the road. "It's a shame they don't prune their trees and spray a little." He showed her the apple, the size

173

of a hen's egg and distorted by brown lumps, looked it over and tossed it aside. "Maybe Susan will buy the place," he said, sweeping his arm out, "and really fix it up."

"It would cost a fortune."

"I heard Barett say her trust fund payments are going way up on her twenty-eighth birthday."

"Are you serious? She could afford to buy a place like this?"

"Well, maybe not for cash, but she could probably work something out."

Deanie could hardly believe what he was saying. "I knew that Susan's father had set up some sort of a trust fund for her, and I know that she gets checks in the mail every so often, but I had no idea that she would actually be coming into so much money so soon."

"She's *never* had to worry about money, and after September she won't even have to *think* about it." He picked another apple, examined it, and tossed it aside. "But she still wants to prove herself, show that she can do it on her own."

"What's wrong with that?"

"Nothing. Nothing at all. Did it sound like I was saying that?"

Deanie kicked a stone up the road and stuck her hands into her pockets. "I guess not. I've just got a lot on my mind."

"About doing it on your own?"

"Of course. You know—like Otis Redding says...'can't do what ten people tell me to do...'"

"I know the feeling. 'Sittin' on the dock of the bay...watchin' the tide roll away...'" He put his arm around her shoulders and kicked another stone up the road.

After a few yards she kicked the same stone up ahead.

Before long they came into the clearing where the pits Zerk had been digging gaped in the sun. Walking across the oval track and between the first two pits Deanie saw that the one on the far end had been backfilled. She couldn't see anything in the next one. The one on her immediate left, in front of the crane, appeared to be half-full of water with a light-gray sediment. The pit to her right, on the other side of Zerk, held a foot or two of bluish sludge that had hardened on the surface and cracked like old custard, and lying in the far corner was the bloated carcass of a raccoon.

They kept walking past scrub oak and sassafras. As they started into the big curve in the path that opened out into Iris's yard, Deanie heard a siren and put her hand on Zerk's forearm. They didn't run, but, as the siren grew louder, it seemed like they were running. Around the last stand of pines she could see it all: cars and vans parked all along the driveway from left to right and back again on the other side; flying hair and hands under the basketball goal; several large tables set up in the yard, people all around them; Barett and Gary on the porch, holding the door while Iris and a girl in a two-piece bathing suit rolled out the upright piano; somebody she didn't recognize suspended from hair, tuning an electric guitar; a badminton bird looping over the net, fanned by rackets; a strawberry roan high-stepping past the corner of the house, Carl Peterson tall in the saddle; dirty-faced Albert up on his hind legs, dancing around like a circus poodle; and pulling in from the road, a big white ambulance with flashing red lights.

At the sight of the ambulance Deanie felt her stomach tighten—but nobody that she could see seemed to be concerned.

"The ambulance crew isn't in any big rush," Zerk said. "It's not an emergency."

She knew he had said that to calm her, but that could also mean that the victim was dead. Now she saw a young woman with long, brown hair, and deep-set dark eyes walking down to meet the ambulance crew standing by the white and gold cab.

"Looks like a false alarm," Zerk said, resting back on the fender of a car.

The woman said something to the driver, the driver reached into the cab, pulled out the radio mike, said something, and put it back. She handed the young woman a clipboard and a pen, apparently for a signature, and climbed back into the cab. Her partner got in the other side, stuck her arm out the window and stared in the direction of the volleyball game.

One of Iris's friends came up, wiping his hands on an oily rag. "Happy birthday, Zerk."

"Thanks."

"What happened?" Deanie asked.

"Some guy was showing off on the ride-around lawn mower and he banged his bare foot between the blade cover and a little tree by the garage"—he gestured with his thumb—"over there where I was working on my car, and his wife"—he gestured towards the ambulance with his other thumb—"freaked out and called the meat wagon."

Deanie watched the driver backing the ambulance out. The red lights were still flashing, and as the sun glinted on the windshield she recalled the mirrored windows in Randall's studio—only here she saw young women on the other side of the glass, and they seemed to be in control of what they were doing. She didn't want to be an ambulance driver, but in a sense she did want to drive more, to take the wheel of her own life, and as she watched the young woman backing the ambulance into the road, she felt that some shadow of herself was lying in the back on a stretcher, looking through a stack of course offerings and travel brochures as though to show some other shadow of herself that she was too much of the time just going along for the ride.

"Kojo's here," Zerk said. He sounded pleased, a little surprised. He pointed towards the picnic table nearest the porch where Kojo and several others sat, talking and gesturing. On the porch two loudspeakers started blasting Donovan's "Mellow Yellow" across the yard.

"You're a popular guy," she said, giving him a poke in the ribs. "Kojo made time to come and wish you a happy birthday."

"I think Iris's *parties* are pretty popular," he said. "Want a beer?"

"Not yet."

"Then I'm going to take a ride on Iris's bike, and see if I can tell what's wrong with it. I'll be around," he said.

"I hope so," she said. "Be careful."

Deanie walked up towards the house and watched Zerk walking around the volleyball players towards the front yard where Carl Peterson rode the horse around slowly in the shade, the brim of his tipped-back western hat brushing from time to time the lower leaves of the maple tree.

"Pretty horse, isn't she?" Terence said. He was strolling up in his western outfit, his hat level, looking serious.

"She sure is. Is she from the farm across the road?"

"Yup." He smiled and brushed the ends of his mustache. "As soon as Carl saw their horses for rent sign, he went right up and rented her for the day."

"And they let him bring her over here?"

"I went along, and the lady there knows me, so she let us take her. And I said we'd currycomb her if they were busy when we brought her back."

The ex-boxer from the Shamrock leaped up from the volleyball players and slammed the ball over the net to the ground in front of a dark-haired woman in a gray granny dress.

"Hey!" he shouted, shaking his fist in the air. "I'm hotter 'n a three-peckered billy goat."

"And twice as smelly," the woman yelled.

"There sure are a lot of people here," Deanie said. There were people from the Shamrock, the university, people she thought she'd seen before, and people she'd never seen before.

Terence nodded. "Iris really got the word out."

"Deanie!" Kojo was calling to her. Arnold Moskey and some students were still at the picnic table, and now Randall Burkhart was sitting with them. "Come and join us."

"Come on, Terence."

"In a while. I'm going to see how Carl's doin' with the horse." He took off towards the front of the house, and Deanie saw Susan driving in between the rows of parked cars. She watched her go past the garage and pull over to park in front of a beat-up Volkswagen van. Deanie started towards Kojo's table and saw Zerk coasting in from the road on Iris's motorcycle. He

177

shut it off, pushed it between the first two parked cars to a spot in the front yard by the forsythia hedge, and disappeared on the other side of Carl Peterson past the front corner of the house. As she came up to Kojo's table she got a whiff of the cooking hamburgers and saw Iris standing by the grill, making a crazy face. Behind her on the porch deck were gifts people had brought for Zerk.

Deanie smiled at Randall, Arnold, her friend Shelley, and sat by Kojo. Shelley was picking at the collar of her yellow blouse, and the other two girls and two guys, all in colored T-shirts, were fooling with plastic cups. While Arnold and Randall argued about something, Deanie leaned towards Kojo. "Any luck getting the notebook?"

"Susan said she'd bring it. She was supposed to bring it back from the city yesterday." He was wearing shades, a gray polo shirt with three-quarter-length sleeves, and jeans. "She just got here," he said.

"I know," Deanie said, "I saw her driving in."

"You talk about the benefits of automation," Arnold was saying to Randall, "but robots don't buy cars." His white, short-sleeved shirt was the kind you could see through, and Deanie could see his undershirt and a book of matches in his pocket.

Randall sighed and took a drink of his whiskey and soda. "What the hell have they been training all the graduate students to do?" He slouched forward and scratched his chest through his green polo shirt.

"To become graduate faculty," Arnold Moskey said, holding a match up to his pipe, "and teach more graduate students."

"I can't stand it," Randall said.

"It has to change," Arnold said. "Some of us know that."

"That's sort of a betrayal—isn't it?" Shelley said. "When my older brother—"

"Ask Kojo about betrayal," Randall said, cutting her off. "It's a major pastime in Africa."

"What do you mean, Shelley?" Deanie asked.

"You're sort of offering somebody something that isn't there—a job, a chance to move up."

"Offering somebody something that isn't there"—Kojo laughed—"you should ask our advertising man about that."

"Wait a minute," Randall said, "you can't lump advertising in with stealing national treasuries and throwing elections."

"Why not? I'm talking about betrayal as a break in trust or belief. I don't care if it's a very thin break, a disappointment of sorts, or a large break, a leader betraying a country."

"Come on, Professor," Randall said, looking around the table, "you've got betrayal on the brain." He leaned across and tapped the table in front of Shelley. "Where he's from they grow up under the influence of a trickster-god—he can't help talking that way." Randall smiled as if he had gained a point in a game. Kojo turned to Deanie and chuckled. "As a matter of fact," Randall went on, "when Kojo fixes himself an egg, he doesn't crack the shell—he betrays it." He slapped the edge of the table and laughed.

Kojo chuckled briefly and stood up.

"Going for some fresh air?" Arnold Moskey asked.

"The cavalry is coming," Kojo said.

"*What's* coming?" Deanie asked.

"Carl Peterson on his horse."

"I thought you said 'Calvary is coming,'" Deanie said. She smiled and then frowned towards Shelley, amused and then puzzled by her mistake, and flipped her hair back over her shoulders.

"I'm getting up to let the horse have my place so Randall can try out some of his pet theories on her," Kojo said.

Randall sat back and sighed, and they all looked up at Carl Peterson and the strawberry roan as they slowly came up to the table. Kojo stepped over the bench, and Deanie saw Susan in her tan culottes and sleeveless top walking up the flagstones towards the house. "Good luck," Deanie said, hoping she had brought the notebook. Kojo raised his eyebrows above his shades and nodded. Across the flagstones, at the picnic table by the side of the porch, Deanie saw the carpenter's helper in a long-sleeved red-plaid shirt sitting by himself, looking in her direction. She smiled and fluttered her hand in a little wave of recognition, and he lifted his hand to his chin, tipped his head a little, and smiled.

"Who's first?" Carl asked. He dismounted and stood by the table, his tan shirt hanging out over his jeans. "Come on, Deanie, how about a ride?"

"Maybe in a while."

"How about you?" He was looking at Shelley. His pale-blue eyes sparkled. Shelley glanced at Deanie. "Come on. It's a nickel for girls with jeans; girls with skirts go free." Shelley smiled and folded her arms on the table.

"That's a deal," Randall said.

"Why don't you give Dean Moskey a ride?" Shelley asked.

"I'm charging men five bucks, and I doubt he'd want to pay that much. Besides, these guys from Brooklyn don't know anything about horseback riding."

Arnold puffed his pipe, looked over his glasses at Carl, and smiled. "Tell me, Carl, how did you come to that conclusion?" he said. Carl laughed and waved off his question and motioned for Shelley to come up for a ride.

Shelley patted her dark curls and looked at Deanie. "Shall I?"

"Go ahead," Deanie said.

Shelley got up. "What's her name?"

"Strawberry," Carl said. "She's gentle and patient—just like I am." He stroked the horse's neck. "That's a pretty skirt you're wearing."

"Thanks," Shelley said. "I had it in my bag and I just put it on under the table so I could get a free ride." Shelley looked at Deanie and laughed.

"A woman of action," Carl said. He adjusted his hat.

"No funny stuff," Shelley said, starting around the table, the short denim skirt tight across her thighs.

"Wouldn't think of it," Carl said. "Here, Randall, hold these a minute." He handed the reins to Randall, got behind Shelley, and put his hands on her waist.

"Be careful, Carl," Randall said, "or you'll be too tired to play with your grandchildren when you get home." Deanie smiled and Arnold chuckled.

"You keep out of this," Carl said.

Deanie knew that Shelley was a good rider and that she could handle herself with Carl.

"Now what are you going to do?" Shelley asked.

"I'm going to hoist you into the saddle." Strawberry snorted and stomped.

Carl stood behind Shelley. "Okay," he said, "grab the saddle horn with your left hand." He clamped his hands around her waist and bent at the knees. "One, two, three." He grimaced, grunted, and straightening his knees, slid her yellow blouse up, away from her skirt.

"Be careful," Shelley said, "or you'll push my blouse right over my head." She winked at Deanie and rolled her eyes for the benefit of the others at the table.

Carl laughed and adjusted his hat with both hands. "God forbid," he said. Deanie noticed a slight nervous ripple at the corner of his mouth—it looked like Shelley might have flustered him a bit.

"Now what?" Shelley asked.

"Better put your foot in the stirrup," Carl said. "Okay, now—one, two, three."

Shelley pulled on the saddle horn, Carl strained at her waist, and lifting herself a little, she threw out her right leg, and flexed her left knee a couple of times. "I'm slipping," she said.

Carl grunted, took a step back, and she slid down against him. "Back to the drawing board," he said.

"Why not get up on the table?" Randall asked. He moved his tall drink aside to make room.

"You stay out of this," Carl said.

Shelley grinned at Deanie and stroked the horse's nose. The horse tossed her head and seemed to steady herself, as if preparing for the next attempt at mounting. Deanie saw Terence coming up behind Carl.

"Need any help?" Terence asked.

"You can help Randall hold the reins if you want to."

"He's doing all right," Terence said. "Strawberry's used to holding still for all the customers across the road—she'll hold still for anybody." He sat down next to Deanie. "How are you doing?"

"Okay. Have you seen Kojo?"

"He and Susan are up in the kitchen discussing world affairs."

Deanie saw Zerk walking along the porch. He glanced through the screen door, came down the steps, walked over to Barett and said something to him. Barett dug into his shirt pocket for a cigarette, and looked over his shoulder towards the kitchen door. Iris came out with several bags of hamburger buns, carried them to the end of the porch, and set them down where they were within arm's reach of the smoking barbecue grill.

"Tell you what, Carl," Shelley said, "why don't you get down behind me and boost me up on your hand?" She put her hands on her hips. "Sort of like a classy waiter with something special."

"I'll give it a try," Carl said, loudly. He glanced at Terence and chuckled. Arnold was looking over his glasses, puffing his pipe, and the others seemed to be watching with interest. The young woman next to Arnold got up, shaking an empty beer can, yawned, and walked away.

Shelley reached for the saddle horn and lifted her foot to the stirrup. "Ready?"

"Just about." Carl appeared to be a little flustered. Now he wasn't looking at anybody. He wiped both hands up and down his pants as if to dry them of sweat, crouched behind Shelley, and pushed the palm of his hand against her rear end.

182

"One, two, three," Shelley said. His arm trembled, his face flushed from the neck, and as he brought his other hand up to push, Shelley let go of the saddle horn. "I'm slipping," she said. Her foot came out of the stirrup and, heels hitting the grass, arms whirling like windmill blades, she backpedaled against Carl, and Carl backpedaled furiously, trying to keep his balance, and five yards from the table they went over backwards—Carl flat on his back, Shelley sitting on his chest.

As Carl lifted his head from his flattened hat, Shelley rocked forward on her hands and knees to get up. "Oh-my-god," he said. His head trembled a moment, fell back into his hat, and he threw his arms out from his sides. "I've died and gone to heaven."

Shelley reached back to her hip, pushed her skirt down over her bare butt, and leaned forward to stand up. She extended her hand to Carl, he reached up, and she helped him to his feet. He looked her in the eye for a moment, picked up his flattened hat, punched the crown out, and from the corner of his eye glanced towards the table.

"If you don't mind, Carl," Shelley said, "I'm going to go see what's going on with the musicians." A trio was playing—piano, bass, and drums—and about a dozen people were sitting on the grass, listening.

"Go ahead," Carl said, laughing, "I'm going to sit down for a minute and catch my breath."

"Ask them if they can play 'Silver Threads Among the Gold' for Carl," Randall said.

"Stick it," Carl said. He picked up Randall's drink and drained it in five throbbing gulps. Randall's mouth fell open and Terence got up and Carl took his place. Terence mounted Strawberry and very smartly reined her up to step backwards six or seven times. He smiled, swept his hat out in a gesture of farewell, and galloped down past the basketball game and onto the barely visible path that curved through the weeds and ran back to the pits.

*   *   *

Deanie stood up to go see what Iris and the birthday boy were doing. Randall had gone back to the city, saying that he had a hot date and he'd see her Wednesday at the next modeling session. Now Deanie was at the food table with a handful of potato chips, looking for the dip.

"I hope she gives the notebook back without making a fuss," somebody said.

Startled, she turned to see Carl Peterson standing there, frowning and looking from side to side as if expecting trouble.

"What kind of a fuss?" she whispered.

"Well"—he filled his cup—"I can't say much about Susan, but let's face it, if she wanted to make enough noise she could get Kojo's ass thrown on the next boat to his motherland."

"I never thought about that."

"It may be a factor," he said. "I know what *I'd* do if she wouldn't give back *my* notebook." He set his jaw and squinted towards the kitchen. Deanie started to tell him that Susan probably wouldn't want his notebook, but, on reflection, it occurred to her that if in some way, in some part of what she was doing, she was trying, subconsciously even, to make herself more interesting to Barett, then she might even want a notebook that belonged to Carl Peterson. "I'm going to get my horse," he said. She saw Terence walking Strawberry on the lawn on the other side of the badminton game as Carl headed down the flagstones.

*   *   *

Hearing screams, Deanie dropped the hamburger back on the grill, and bumped into Iris as they both turned to see. Above the badminton players Deanie saw the woman in the granny dress riding backwards on Carl Peterson's shoulders, her dress over his head, her heels pounding his kidneys. He stumbled blindly into the players, his hat stuck on his foot like an overshoe, and as she screamed and beat on his head, he turned like a top and spun into the badminton net bringing the whole thing to the ground in a flurry of arms and feet.

Next to the house stood Strawberry, a tipped-over lawn chair at her side.

"I'm not even gonna bother going down there," Iris said.

Deanie lifted the hamburger she had dropped and put it on a bun.

"Would you hold these a second?" Iris said. She tapped Deanie's arm and held out a tray of hamburger patties. "Albert's got his eye on 'em." Albert sat in the grass by the table, his nose up, sniffing the meat. "I'll make a few more burgers and then bring out the cake. This batch will finish five dozen hamburgers." Iris giggled with delight. "Can you believe that?"

Deanie nodded. "Have you seen Susan lately?" She set the tray on the porch.

"Yeah. She went for a walk down the road a while ago." Iris pointed towards the road in front of the house.

Deanie looked across the yard towards the road. There were still quite a few people waiting around for the cake. Barett was holding Gary up to admire Strawberry, Zerk was playing volleyball. "Do you know where Kojo is?" she asked.

"He's around"—Iris pressed the grease from a couple of hamburgers and pulled the turner up from the flames—"Susan's around, Barett's around"—she squashed another hamburger— "are you worried about something?"

"No, maybe I was—" Deanie saw the carpenter's helper looking at her from a picnic table where he sat across from another fellow whose back was to her. She smiled.

"Maybe you were what?"

"I don't know." Deanie looked back towards the carpenter's helper and saw him approaching, his hands in his pockets. "Hello, Larry," she said.

"Hi."

"Do you want a hamburger?"

"Sure."

"He's had three already," Iris said, laughing.

"Have you?"

He blushed. "I guess so."

Deanie gave him a hamburger. "Are you having a good time?"

"Yeah," he said. "I played some volleyball and took a look at the training grounds an' stuff like that."

"Training grounds?" Iris said.

"For Zerk's school," Deanie said. "The sample basements..."

"That's right," Iris said. "The pits. How could I forget?"

"Do you know many people here, Larry?" Deanie asked.

"No. Basically just you." He smiled, looked down, and rubbed the side of his neck.

"This is Iris"—Deanie glanced around—"and this is Larry. Now you know *two* people here."

"And here comes Terence," Iris said, as Terence rode up on Strawberry.

Larry looked up at Terence. "Nice horse," he said, nodding and rubbing the horse's neck. "Pretty girl." He smiled at Deanie and walked back to the table.

* * *

"She wants a ceremony," Kojo said. He let go of the screen door and rested his arm over the top of the upright piano.

"A ceremony?" Deanie had been standing at the piano, working out some blues chords while one of the musicians strummed a chord now and then on his guitar. She played six more chords and stuck her hands into her back pockets. The musician lit a cigarette and began packing up his equipment. "Susan wants a ceremony?"

Kojo raised his eyebrows and nodded. "She wants to go back to the clearing and stand under the moon and burn the lists of names."

"She's not acting like she was last week at the Shamrock—is she?"

"No, I don't think so," Kojo said, "and you've talked to her, haven't you?"

"Yes, but that was earlier." She looked around and saw Susan at one of the tables, pouring a soda for Gary. "She seems to be having a good time. She looks all right."

"Did you say anything to her about the notebook?"

"No," Deanie said. "The way it looked the two of you had everything worked out"—she paused—"finally."

"That was never in doubt." He seemed to laugh under his breath. "What I mean is that as soon as I caught up with her this afternoon she told me right off that she'd brought the notebook and that she would give it back before she left"—he adjusted his sunglasses in his shirt pocket—"and now she wants a ceremony."

"Terence said you and Susan were discussing world affairs in the kitchen."

Kojo laughed. "We were reminiscing—on the surface at least—about people and places in London," he said, lowering his voice, "and Susan may have been tying up some loose ends as to what her knowledge of the lists of good guys and bad guys means to her in"—he shrugged—"in whatever she thinks she's doing."

The musician carried his guitar and amplifier past her, and went down the steps.

"See you later," Deanie said.

"Later."

She frowned and reached out to play a couple of chords in the minor key. "Isn't Susan supposed to come into a lot of money pretty soon?"

"She's supposed to. I'm surprised that she told you."

"She didn't—Zerk told me." Deanie played two more chords. "Do you think she wanted to invest in Ghana?"

Kojo laughed. "Deanie, you're too much."

"Well?" She played a chord.

187

"I think she had illusions." Kojo walked around her to the conga drum standing on the other side of the piano, snapped his fingers in his palms, and tapped on the drum. "But that's really all I can say." Kojo drummed on the conga, Deanie played a chord, he drummed again, she played two chords, he drummed again. "She's talking to Barett now—maybe Barett and Gary are going home."

Deanie turned around and saw Barett and Gary walking away from Susan towards Barett's station wagon. It was just getting dark. "Maybe," she said.

"We'll see," Kojo said, walking past her. He stopped to let Iris come up the steps with a tray of celery and carrots and went down towards Susan.

* * *

"Well, Zerk, how does it feel to be thirty?" Deanie said. They were sitting on the top of a picnic table, their feet on the bench, the remainder of the birthday cake behind them.

"I don't know. How do I feel to you?" Zerk put his arm around her and pulled her close to him.

"You feel pretty good." It was the first time they'd sat down together all day.

After Iris had brought the cake down from the kitchen and fifteen or twenty people had sung "Happy Birthday," and after Zerk had blown out the candles and given everybody a piece of cake, they had all gone up to the porch where Zerk opened his gifts—mostly wine, a few six-packs, a bottle of whiskey, a Superman T-shirt, and a phony ruby ring that squirted water. Gradually the people drifted back to other tables, the interminable basketball game, or into the house, and Zerk and Deanie came back to the table and sat by his cake. Now the two yard lights were on and Deanie glanced up at his eyes and saw that he was staring towards the back of the house. She saw Susan and Kojo cutting through the shadows towards the back of the garage and she felt Zerk's hand tightening around her arm.

Zerk loosened his grip. "I'm sorry," he said. He raised his arms and brought his hands down to the table by his thighs.

"Relax," she said, rubbing her arm. "They're not doing anything."

"Who?"

"I'm not blind," she said. "They're just going back to your clearing to"—she groped for a word—"to clear something up." Zerk sighed and moved to get up. "It's like your birthday cake"—she picked a candle from the cake and held it out—"she wants to do something to mark the end of something. That's all."

Shelley came up to the table carrying a bottle of beer. "Hi, everybody."

"I have to stretch my legs," Zerk said, standing up. He hitched up his jeans and without turning around kept going across the yard, grabbing a beer from a tub of ice water, veering into the shadows.

"Was it something I said?" Shelley asked. She belched and took a drink.

"No," Deanie said. "I just think he can't believe he's thirty."

Shelley shrugged. "Why don't you give him a little birthday hand job," she said, moving her hand up and down her beer bottle, "and make him feel better?"

"You're impossible," Deanie said.

"It's an impossible world, sister. What can I tall ya?" Shelley shrugged again and headed for the house.

Deanie walked down towards the garage, keeping an eye out for Zerk and Susan and Kojo. Somebody had hung a floodlight out of the small window under the peak of the roof, and three people were shooting baskets. The carpenter's helper dribbled twice and held the ball as she approached. She didn't know the other two fellows.

"Hello, Larry."

"Hi."

"Have you seen Zerk?"

"You mean since he was sitting by you?"

189

"Yes." She clicked her thumbnail on her tooth.

"No," he said. "Is something wrong?" She shook her head.

"Deanie," Kojo said. He came up to her from the driveway, between the parked cars.

"What?"

"Will you come with us?"

"Come with you?" she said, frowning. "Why?"

"Just come along—please," his eyebrows went way up and he nodded vigorously. "I can't see your expression in the dark," he said. "Are you frowning?" He moved to the side and she turned a little towards the light. She saw Larry and his two friends standing there, staring, and she turned back from the light. "Please," he said.

"Does Susan want me to come along?" she whispered.

"She won't mind."

It seemed strange that they would want somebody to come along, but at the same time she kept recalling Carl Peterson's comment about how easy it would be to get an alien sent back to his homeland. She didn't think Susan would make any crazy accusations to get Kojo in trouble—but at the same time she knew that she herself wasn't looking at the world through Kojo's eyes. She flipped her hair over her shoulders. Kojo stopped nodding and took a step towards the driveway. "Let's go," she whispered.

Deanie followed him. The sky was clear, the air still, and the floodlight sparkled on the windows of the cars. They walked past three cars, and Kojo stopped to open the rear door of his little car for her. Susan was in the front seat, smoking a cigarillo.

"Hello, Susan," Deanie said.

"Aren't you excited?" Susan asked.

"Excited?"

"About the ceremony."

Kojo started the car, clicked on the headlights, and pulled onto the dirt driveway that faded into two tracks through the weeds up ahead.

"Kojo didn't say much about it."

Susan punched out the cigarillo and held up something. "Can you see this, Deanie?"

"No."

"Does your dome light work?" she said to Kojo.

"No," Kojo said. "There should be a flashlight in the glove box."

Susan found the flashlight. "This is Kojo's notebook, and"—she tore out a page—"these are the lists. And we're going to build a fire and burn them up." She shut off the flashlight, found a radio station that was playing something with violins and harps, and sat back.

Deanie watched the headlights shaping a tunnel through the scrub oak and pine. She watched the light catching the white birches, how they shone in the woods like the bleached skeleton of a huge bird—till the light fanned out over the pits and around Zerk's crane.

"Park over there," Susan said, tapping on the windshield. She pointed to a level sandy place by a pit near Zerk's drag bucket. On the other side of the pit sat the red and black crane, the boom projecting up through the light into the darkness. Kojo parked the car. "Let's gather some twigs and sticks for the fire," she said, getting out. "I've got the flashlight. You can help, Deanie, if you want to." Kojo turned off the lights and got out.

Deanie stood by the car, looked at the moon, and tried to find the Big Dipper. "Why did you pick this spot?"

"It looked good this afternoon," she said. "Let's find some sticks." She clicked on the flashlight and shined it towards the trees. Kojo was walking back with a bundle of sticks. "Where did you get those?"

"I just picked them up—I've spent quite a few days of my life gathering firewood."

"Why don't you put them there?" Susan said, shining the light to a spot not far from the car.

Kojo put the sticks down, and the three of them walked into the woods and picked up more sticks. Deanie thought she saw a flashlight blink back on the path from the house—but maybe not.

191

*   *   *

As Deanie watched the flames shrink into embers the darkness around her seemed to thicken, become palpable. After Kojo had got the fire going, Susan had put the page with the lists of names in it, and then Kojo had torn up the notebook and put it on to burn. None of them had said anything during the burning—but their faces had been lit up enough to let Deanie see that Susan looked genuinely sad and at times startled and that Kojo appeared alternately bored and anxious.

In the car again, in the back seat, with all the windows down, and the thick darkness sliding against the car, Deanie thought she saw lights blinking back on the path, closer this time. Maybe they were fireflies. Susan turned on the radio. Or maybe the volleyball players were playing hide-and-seek.

"Shall we go?" Kojo asked.

"I don't see why we shouldn't," Susan said.

"Are you sure you don't want to burn something else?" Kojo said.

"Are you making fun of me?"

"No. I just thought I'd ask before we go back." Kojo started the car, backed a few feet and jerked to a stop.

"You can buy your guns yourself," Susan said.

"What's this?" he said.

Deanie heard the whine of the starter motor on the crane, and the diesel engine rumbled like the rolling of a tremendous drum, and the spotlight came full into their faces from across the pit.

"Oh-my-god," Susan said, "what's Zerk *doing*?"

"The car won't move," Kojo said. He tried to back it—it stalled, and began moving forward towards the pit. He put it in neutral and pulled on the emergency brake. The crane roared. The car kept moving towards the pit. Deanie saw people from the party standing off to the right in the edge of light from the headlights. Some of them were carrying flashlights. The car kept moving. "He's got us on a bloody cable."

192

"Those people are *watching*," Susan said.

"There are too many witnesses," Kojo said. "He couldn't—"

The car jerked and banged down hard and tipped way up and Deanie fell back in the seat, feeling her stomach weightless an instant, papers falling down in her face from the glove box, the engine roaring, now idling, and down below the back window splashes from things falling sparkled in the water, and they were all cheering and applauding, she couldn't believe it, and as the car swung with the turning crane the windshield flashed white from a humming electrical sparking on the boom hitting the wires and she saw the horse and rider galloping past the cheering onlookers to the crane, bursting all blue to snap electrically half a dozen times like a flag in a sudden gust of wind.

Now the water was everywhere, no more air pockets, her lungs hurting for air, and she felt the arm strong around her waist, the hand gripping her shoulder, turning her, pulling her over the seat, pushing her up through the window, through water to air, the screams.

The smell of burnt hair made her gag. She couldn't look past the people standing by the crane. Kojo pulled her to her feet, and they stood on the top of the submerged car, waist deep in water.

Deanie clamped her hand over her nose and mouth, and holding Kojo's arm, she felt his arm pressing tight to his chest as if he was in deep pain. "Are you okay?" she said.

"I think so."

She glanced towards the people, the wobbling flashlights. For an instant she saw part of the saddle and the horse's neck flat in the weeds. "Was Terence on the horse?" she said.

"I don't know," he whispered. He wheezed and doubled over.

"Are you okay?" she said.

"I'll be all right." He came up slowly, holding his chest.

"Is the rider..."

"He's dead."

"Oh-no-no-no-no." She caught her breath. "Where's Susan?"

"She's up there." The spotlight was pointing across the bank towards the trees. She saw Susan standing back from the caved-in edge of the bank.

"She jumped out before we went up"—he doubled over—"I got tangled up and fell."

Somebody came past Susan with a ladder and slid it down into the water next to the car.

Deanie turned her face into Kojo's shoulder. "Thank you." She was crying. He reached up and held her.

At the top of the ladder she recognized the ex-boxer from the Shamrock. "Was it Terence? Was Terence on the horse?" she said.

"No"—he paused, helping her off the ladder—"they said it was some kid named Larry."

Deanie went numb. After a moment everything around her throbbed and receded from her and came back mixed-up and confused. She grabbed the ladder and shook it, and seeing Susan coming towards her she lunged for her, catching her arm, pulling it. "Why? Why did you?" she screamed. Her other hand went for Susan's face and the ex-boxer stepped between them. Deanie pushed at his shoulders, immovable, and sliding her hands down she gathered his shirt into her fists and buried her face in his chest.

TWELVE

Deanie lay watching dust particles floating in the thin planes of sunlight sliding past the drapes. She pulled the sheet up and looked for a moment at her wet clothes on the bathroom floor, the muddy sneakers under the window where she had stood staring at the stars last night. She didn't know how long she had stood there, thinking of Larry, wishing she could start yesterday all over again. She hadn't been able to sleep more than a few minutes from time to time all night.

She reached out and opened the door a few inches. Zerk was asleep on the sofa. She wondered where her clock was. She saw it. It was almost nine.

Deanie pulled on a robe and went into the living room. Zerk was lying on his side, his knees drawn up, his head on a chair cushion. He was still wearing the headband she had given him, and he had pulled her beach blanket across his shoulders. She stood there, watching him breathe, wondering how everything had happened. Her gut reaction had been to blame Susan for having something to do with Zerk's stunt—and then she felt rotten for thinking that Zerk would have anything to do with trying to hurt someone. And then when Zerk said he'd only been crawling around in the dark to see what would happen, she wondered, for *what*? To see if at the age of thirty he could still pull off something that would get him a lot of attention, and in front of a bunch of people running around in the woods with flashlights? But maybe there was more to it, she didn't know. She did know that Larry's ride to save her from harm had ended in a horrible accident. And with a chill she wondered what she could have done differently to have prevented him from being attracted to her. Was that *her* fault? And why had she been so quick to blame Susan last night? But, she didn't know. She didn't know anything. No, that wasn't true. What did she know? She knew that she could still go to Palermo, Oklahoma, if she wanted to. That much she knew.

Making a pot of tea and slicing and toasting a bagel had taken Deanie some real effort, even with Zerk helping. Now she was at the small kitchen table, watching Zerk at the stove, grilling himself a bacon, peanut butter, and mayonnaise sandwich.

"Tell me again," Deanie said, "last night's not very straight in my head."

"Well, do you remember telling the cops off?" Zerk said.

"Yes—sort of."

"But you don't remember Kojo telling the ambulance crew that he was okay?" She shook her head. "And the cops taking me to the police station?" She shook her head.

"And here I am," Zerk said. He flipped the sandwich over and took a drink of his ginger ale.

"And Larry will never be here again," she said. She took a deep breath and slowly exhaling stared out the window.

"I know," he said.

"You're sure Kojo's all right?"

"Yes. He said he was okay. And I told him how it happened, and I told him I was sorry," Zerk said.

Deanie stared at Zerk. "What did he say then?"

"He just nodded," Zerk said, "and he said 'All right, Zerk, I'm going back to my apartment.'"

Deanie stared at Zerk, and he frowned. "Look," he said, a little defensively, it seemed, "the *bank* gave way. I was just going to pull the car a *few feet* with the drag line. That's all. When the bank gave way my lift line to the bucket kept the car from dropping right into the pit. And for the tenth time, I didn't know you were in the car, and brushing the power line was no real problem until the kid on the horse came charging up and leaned against the crane."

"He saw me get into the car," Deanie said. "He knew I was in it. He was trying to save me."

"I know. I know that," Zerk said.

"Did you tell everybody to follow you out there?"

"No, not exactly. I mean it wasn't a secret. As I said, I was just gonna crawl around in the dark and see what happened. For all I know, Larry told 'em to go back there." Zerk put the sandwich on a dish and sat at the table.

Deanie put her head in her hands. She was having trouble focusing. "Won't there be some sort of investigation?"

"There'll probably be a coroner's report in a couple of weeks and then an inquest in a couple of months," Zerk said. "Shouldn't amount to much."

Deanie put her head in her hands. She was afraid to ask about Susan and Iris. No, she remembered, Susan was okay. Kojo said she had jumped out in time. She remembered she had yelled at Susan and pushed her, how could she have forgotten that? "What did Iris do?" She looked up.

"I don't know," he said, crumpling his soda can. He tipped back in his chair and appeared to be looking around for a place to shoot a basket. Deanie grabbed the can and put it on the table next to her teacup. Zerk mimicked a set shot in slow motion, tipped the chair forward, and brought his hands floating to his lap like falling leaves. Now, whatever he had been holding off caught him and he dropped his face into his hands, and as Deanie put her head on his shoulder she saw the tears running down the inside of his forearm.

* * *

Now Deanie was sitting at the table with Zerk. They had been there for quite a while it seemed, not talking, just glancing at each other and looking out the window at the clear sky. She knew they had to move around, do something. "Let's walk down to the beach," she said.

Zerk lifted his arms and stretched. "That's probably a good idea," he said. "Some fresh air and some fresh water can't hurt."

* * *

She dives through her shadow and kicks till her stretching arms brush rocky bottom and sweep back in the cool dull weight of water. Her hands slide past her ribs to thrust a breast stroke obliquely down from her rising chin and she breaks surface to stand and lift away from her shadow now spreading over the crystal flints of water. The fresh air feels sharp in her nose and she exhales hard and long and pulls her dripping hair back over her ears and holds it tight to her neck as she moves towards shore watching her shadow grow away from her waist, her thighs, her knees on the water. Now the water is calf-deep and she turns and sits and fans out her arms and stretches her legs way out and watches how her jeans want to float away from her legs in the rippling water, how her toes want to float away from her feet, how the glints of light want to float away from the sun.

Zerk has been sitting in the water where she left him, before she went for a swim. He's leaning back on his elbows, watching her. She cups her hand and sends a wave rolling towards him, and he sits up, resting his arms on his knees. Behind him on the shore a man who has been surf-casting is showing a fish to two little girls playing on the beach. Farther back through the dark scrub oak running along the top of the gravelly bank a blinking

amber light marks an intersection in the road that runs past Iris's
house and the Sanborn estate.

"Did you say something?" Zerk said.

"No," she said, realizing that he had been daydreaming or
lost in thought.

"Are you ready to go?" he said.

"If you are," she said, hoping that he felt better, now that
they'd been relaxing in the water for a while, washing away, she
hoped, some of the horror from the night before.

Zerk stood up and reached out to give her a hand. "I'm
going to go away for a while," he said.

"Where?" she said.

"I don't know," he said. "I just have to be alone for a
while."

Deanie started to say that he could go to Palermo,
Oklahoma, with her, but when she saw how withdrawn and
determined he looked she figured that he was already on his way
to someplace and anything she said now would probably upset
him. "Call me," she said.

He nodded and squeezed her hand, and when they got to the
gatehouse he kissed her on the cheek and headed for his place.

*   *   *

*Lying here on the sofa staring at the ceiling. It's after 9:00
p.m. and I just tried to call you, but some guy said you were out.
Who was that? It sounded like Terence. I was too upset to ask.
Maybe it was Terence. What's he doing in your apartment? I
could have watched it for you. It doesn't make any difference. I
feel like somebody hit me in the stomach.*

*I just wanted to hear your voice. I miss you so much. If I
could just feel your hair and touch your cheeks. I hope you're
not in a bar someplace talking to somebody else when you could
be talking to me. But I don't care. I'll be in Italy for nine
months and you'll probably be talking to a lot of somebodies.
Fuck it. I just don't care. But I do.*

Since you walked away yesterday I've been thinking about you and the times we've shared, the walks in the woods, your stories about the all the things you've done. When I walked by Iris's house this morning I thought about Albert chasing everybody out and I even laughed and then I started to cry. I wish I knew what you're doing. I want so much to tell you how much I miss you and how lonely I am. I want to hear you say you love me even if I can't say it to you. I want you to be here so I can tell you that sometimes I don't think I can take it any more. If only I could hold you.

Lying here like this. I just don't know. I'm starting to see faces in the plaster, big eyeballs, pointed teeth. Shit. I've go to do something...get organized...get something done.

*   *   *

The next morning Deanie went to the door thinking she had heard the carpenter, who sometimes came up to use her phone. But no, she thought, it wouldn't be Jacob, he wouldn't be working today. She was wearing only a short terry cloth robe and when she saw Zerk and the flowers she felt a rush of excitement and she could that tell her face was flushed. This morning she had thought that he would be gone for days, and now here he was at her door, holding out a bunch of tiny white and yellow wild flowers.

"Are you okay?" she said.

He nodded. "Yes." He nodded again. "Are you?"

"I am now," she said, stepping back.

Zerk came in and handed her the flowers. "These are for you," he said.

"Thank you," she said. She put her hand to her cheek, her face was still flushed. She wondered what to do with the flowers. "Let me put them in some water." She took the flowers to the kitchen and coming back from the sink she thought he seemed taller than before, standing there in his work boots and jeans, looking at her books and papers spread on the coffee table and all along the sofa.

"Does this mean you're studying for a test or something?" he said.

"Not really," she said. "I'm just trying to get organized for a paper I have to do. I don't want to get behind."

Then it was all over. As soon as he asked if she had to study, she wondered if maybe he was asking if she had something more important to do now than to be with him. Then it was all over. Without hesitating Deanie leaned over the coffee table to clear a space for him on the sofa, and as soon as she leaned over the table her right leg went up for balance, and realizing the position she was in, she lifted her leg a little more and bent her knee a couple of times. When she stood up and turned around Zerk's arms were out to hold her and she could have pushed him over with a feather. She clasped her hands behind his neck and closing her eyes let her mouth fall open to meet his lips and his tongue churning around and around. His arms held her closer and closer and then he was opening her robe and she could feel him hard against her. After a few moments they were on the sofa, their clothes on the floor.

"Do you have protection?" she said.

He sighed. "No," he said, making a sour face, "I guess I'll have to run up to my place."

"I'll see if I can find something," she said, getting up from the sofa. "The pill makes me gain weight so I had to stop taking them for a while. The camera doesn't lie."

"That's what they say."

She found her bag and as she looked in it for a condom she wondered why he didn't have one with him. Had he not been planning to make love to her? Or did he think he could get by without one? Could he be that thoughtless? But then, he hadn't known that she'd stopped taking the pill. Why was she thinking this way? she wondered. She found a condom and turned back to the living room. Zerk was sitting there, his arms thrown out along the back of the sofa, and clenched in his teeth—the stem of a single pink and white flower.

THIRTEEN

Susan had called a little earlier and now Deanie was on her way up to the mansion to have a cup of tea with her. As she walked through the early dark past Zerk's place she saw that his car was gone and figured that he was shooting pool at the Shamrock. She wondered how Kojo was doing. He'd gone to Newark to visit his cousins, that much she'd heard from Linda—but that didn't tell her how he was mending from everything that had happened Saturday night. The remembrance of it all moved her with a shudder—Kojo had saved her life...and Larry had lost his. She thought she was handling it pretty well—she wasn't going to the funeral...she had hardly known him at all...and nobody could really know whether he'd really been trying to save her...it was just the best explanation...but...she started to cry...there was so much...to deal with. She stopped a moment, wiped her cheeks, and took a deep breath. She swung her foot through the grass by the side of the drive and continued up towards the mansion. The sand felt good on her feet and when she came to the crushed rock she walked on the grass and breathed deeply of the smell of cut sweet clover blowing from the hay field across the road. As she came up to the house she could hear a Brahms flute concerto and through the window she saw Barett in his stuffed chair, reading. The kitchen light was on. Susan was sitting on the porch, framed by the screen door behind her.

"Hi, Deanie," Susan said. "That's a nice breeze, isn't it?"

"Yes, you can smell the clover from across the road." Susan looked relaxed in her shorts and sleeveless top.

"I didn't expect you here so soon, I haven't made any tea yet."

"That's okay."

Susan crossed her legs and clasped her hands over her knee, and Deanie noticed how the forsythia in front of the window cast squiggly shadows across Susan, the corner of the porch, and her jeans, as though someone had dropped a net over them, and she took a step back as if to disentangle herself.

"Have you seen Kojo?" Susan asked.

"No," she said. "He's gone to Newark to visit his cousins."

"Is that Deanie?" Barett asked through the screen door. She hooked her thumbs over her jeans, shifted her weight to one foot, and watched him come out. "Hello, Deanie," he said. "How are you doing?"

"All right."

"Did you ask her?" Barett said, bending towards Susan.

"She just got here," Susan said. Barett stuck a hand into his pants pocket and pulled at his beard. "We were wondering if you would take Gary with you when you go into the city Wednesday. Unless you're going to the funeral."

"No," Deanie said. She looked over Susan and past Barett into the empty kitchen. "I'm not going to the funeral, though I keep getting the feeling that I'm on the horse riding with him, that he's still riding the horse and I'm riding with him to the grave." She kept looking into the empty kitchen and after a moment she told herself that they weren't going to respond to what she'd said. "Why do you want me to take him?"

"He'd enjoy going with you and the three of us could use a little breathing space," Barett said.

Deanie looked up at the stars around the edge of the mansion roof thinking it might be good for Gary to get away for a while, and he'd probably have fun spending half a day in the studio, and, for a moment, she wished she could just take off and wake up on the beach somewhere with Zerk—after all, she needed some breathing space too.

"You *are* going in to your modeling session, aren't you?" Susan asked.

"Yes," Deanie said. "I can take him along. Aren't you going in this week?"

Susan shook her head, uncrossed her legs, and rubbed her knees. "I'm going to be working at home," she said. "I'm trying to finish up a couple of projects."

"Is it okay if I use your car once in a while?" Deanie asked.

"Of course, just take it whenever you need it. You know where the keys are. I can take the station wagon if anything comes up."

Deanie waited for Barett to make something out of Susan's remark, and when he didn't, she was a little surprised. She wondered if he felt as worn-out as she herself did, or if everything that had happened in the last three days had in some way tempered his linguistic imperialism. The phrase took her back to that afternoon at the West End, and she wished she knew what Kojo was doing now.

"Speaking of cars," Barett asked, "what's the story with Dedu's car? The seats must be a little damp."

"It's just sitting there," she said. "Zerk hauled it out of the water."

"I didn't think he drove his own car to Newark," Barett said.

"What of it?" Susan said.

"I don't think he walked to Newark," Barett said.

"He could have called one of his friends at the U. N.," Deanie said. "But, as Susan said, 'What of it?'"

"Time will tell," Barett said. He bit at the end of his mustache and, shaking his fist in front of his face, appeared to be talking to himself as he turned and went inside. It looked like he was really getting wound up about finding out what Kojo did when he wasn't around Peeze, and she wasn't going to say anything that would get Barett started on speculating about what he imagined Kojo was doing with Susan or anybody else.

She saw that Susan was staring into the darkness, apparently lost in thought, and she looked down the drive towards the road. She wondered how Iris and Terence were feeling, what they were doing, and now as she watched Susan staring off into the darkness she realized that she hadn't really apologized for yelling at her Saturday night. "Susan?" Susan looked up. "I'm sorry I acted like you had something to do with Zerk's"—she paused—"what Zerk did."

"Forget it," she said. "In your state of mind," she hesitated, looked away, and looked back at her, "just forget it."

"Thanks. I'm sorry," Deanie said.

"Don't be sorry, be Deanie." Susan pulled a cigarillo from the shadows and lit it.

Deanie watched the smoke roll through the light and lose itself in the darkness. She watched a little swirl of smoke curling back into the light and heard Barett putting on another tape, a string quartet, and for a moment she wondered if Barett was learning anything from Larry's death, if he was listening to Susan any differently, or if he was just holding his tongue because Susan's trust fund payments were going up. "What does Barett think about your trust fund payments going up this fall?"

"Did Kojo tell you that?"

"No."

"It must have been Zerk," Susan said, recrossing her legs and folding her hands on her knee. She yawned—apparently the question hadn't caused her any anxiety. "He hasn't said anything. But why are you asking me that?"

"Just curious," she said, wishing she hadn't asked about the trust fund. "Does Gary know?"

"Know what?"

"That Larry was killed."

"Oh, no," she said, shaking her head, "Gary didn't know him, and he wasn't allowed to play around where they were working. So"—she shrugged and sighed—"we didn't see any need to tell him."

*   *   *

Deanie made sure Gary's seat belt was fastened, and Susan and Barett, waving good-by to Gary, backed away from the car as she swung it into the drive. As she headed towards the road she adjusted the rear-view mirror and saw Susan in her silk housecoat and Barett in his terry cloth bathrobe going up the porch steps.

The early morning sun brought out the yellow and orange in the weeds and the bark of the trees and the new wood paneling around the porch of the gatehouse. She was glad to be getting away on time. The train ran right behind the funeral home, so she would sit on the opposite side with Gary and read to him till they were through Port Jefferson. That way he wouldn't see any familiar faces by the funeral home and ask her what was going on. She heard Gary unwrapping something and smelled bubble gum. He was stuffing a chunk into his mouth. "Have you got one for me?" Deanie asked.

Gary nodded and winked an eye with each exaggerated chew, and pulled a piece of gum from the pocket of his bib overalls. "Here," he said, holding out the gum.

"Thanks." Deanie saw that it wasn't the sugarless gum that Susan favored for him. "Where did you get this?"

Gary smiled and winked and chewed. "My friend Larry gave it to me," he said, turning to his window and tapping on the glass. "He works there under the tree with Jacob." Deanie aimed the car between the gateposts and stopped at the edge of the road, her forehead on the steering wheel, the gum tight in her fist, tears dripping off her nose. "What's the matter?" She shut her eyes, and rolling her head on the steering wheel, felt totally helpless. "Are my teeth going to fall out?"

She took a deep breath and sighed. "No, Gary, your teeth aren't going to fall out." She wiped her nose on her wrist, found a tissue, wiped her wrist, and dabbed her cheeks.

"Why are you crying?"

"I'm crying because Larry's not coming back anymore." Gary frowned and appeared to be waiting for her to continue. "He was in an accident and now he's dead."

Tears welled up in Gary's eyes and his lower lip trembled. Deanie bit her thumbnail, sighed heavily, and nodded.

"Was he in a car?"

"No," she said, pulling onto the road, "he was outside."

"He didn't look both ways?"

She ran it up to forty in low and kept squeezing the bubble gum in her fist. "That's it, Gary." She shifted into drive and handed him a tissue. "He didn't look both ways."

As Deanie slowed for the train station she glanced at Gary. He was blowing a bubble and reading the comics that came wrapped around the gum.

*　　*　　*

Susan came to the door as Gary started up the steps.

"Look what I've got," he said. He held up a bag of candy bars and a small bag of potato chips that some of the models had given him. "*Muchas gracias.*"

"I guess *you* had a good time," Susan said as he pushed past her and disappeared into the house. "Even learned a little Spanish."

"Everybody loved him," Deanie said, holding out the car keys.

"Thanks," Susan said, taking the keys. "Do you want to come in?"

"No, I'm beat. I just want to get back and take a shower."
She couldn't wait to take a shower and have a bowl of soup.
Then, she told herself, she'd go over to Iris's place.

* * *

Heading into the dark woods on the way to Iris's place,
Deanie held the flashlight loosely at her side, the rhythm of her
walking throwing the beam of light in looping streaks that
bumped down the path and skipped back over the blues and
greens of the weeds. She felt a little better now than she did this
morning—taking care of Gary all day had, now that she thought
about it, stopped her from going around in circles about Larry's
death. She heard something and stopped. Nothing. She started
off, the light bumping out and skipping back. She saw the ivy-
covered stone bench by the path, now she was halfway through
the woods. She wanted to see how Iris was feeling... She heard
something crashing through the brush and stopped. She swept
her light through the trees. Nothing. But it was so loud, it
sounded like a horse. She clicked off the light and froze,
straining to see whatever it was in the moonlight. Nothing.
Suddenly she heard herself breathing loud and fast and she
caught a breath, held it, and blew it out in a rush. She clicked on
the light, shook her head back, and then she was jogging towards
Iris's place. As she jogged through the woods, the feeling came
back of a part of her riding to the grave with Larry, and as she
tried to identify some outline, some shape of herself riding off,
she caught across the treetops the fleeting image of what
appeared to be a horse, a horse composed of a beach blanket,
some rolled towels, flying elbows and hair, torn poster pictures
of Naples, a bent pair of mirror-finished sunglasses.

The sight of Zerk's crane across the clearing made her stop.
She waited to see if the spotlight would come on. Nothing. Of
course not, he said he'd be home. She swept the flashlight beam
across the clearing and started across. She saw something
sparkling in the sand. Closer, the sparkles lay in a circle. A

209

diamond necklace. Closer, she saw the ring of broken glass, what was left of a large jar run over by the bulldozer.

She shined her light along the bulldozer tracks in the dirt, saw them crisscrossing, and farther out saw that two more of the pits had been backfilled. She kept on into the last stretch of woods, and as the bridle path opened out into Iris's lawn she saw how the grass, the porch light, the white-clapboard house—the whole scene—seemed flat, almost two-dimensional, since Larry's death.

As Deanie walked up to the porch the sight of the upright piano and the empty conga drum stand reawakened her wondering about Kojo. Why had he gone to Newark? Had he been running from something? Or to something? She began feeling short of breath. Or had he even been running? The yard light came on, and she saw Terence at the screen door watching her approach.

"I've been expecting you," he said. She glanced at the bushes and looked over her shoulder. "You act like you're being followed."

"I hadn't noticed," she said, going up the steps. She was glad to be going inside.

*   *   *

Leaning against the kitchen counter, sipping her wine, Deanie watched Terence sorting through some pages of typing on the table. He was barefoot and wearing faded jeans and a leather vest. His mustache was flat against his cheeks as if he had been pressing it down with a sweaty hand.

"So Iris went home to visit her mother?" Deanie said.

He nodded. "She left last night—around eight-thirty. She put together some pictures the kids in her classes drew last spring to show her mother, stuck three baskets of dirty laundry in the back seat, sat Albert in the passenger seat with a blue and white baby bonnet on his head and took off."

"I would like to have seen her..."

210

"She said she'd be back Sunday night, she's scheduled to work the Monday lunch." He picked up his wine and sat on the corner of the table. "Do you want to call her?"

"No. I'll see her later. I was really looking forward to seeing her tonight." She sipped her wine. "What are you working on?" She waved her hand across the typewriter.

"Oh"—he sighed—"it's a long poem about the last few days, Larry's funeral."

"Were there many people there?"

He shook his head. "Zerk went."

"I know," she said.

"He had the guts to tell Larry's parents that he died a hero," he said.

Deanie didn't know what to say. She could hardly believe that he was writing a poem about the funeral—and he hadn't even gone to it. "Well," she said, after a moment, "I'm going back now."

*   *   *

Deanie stood in front of Zerk's place a few minutes before going in. The apartment was lit only by light from the TV. She could see Zerk's legs sticking out from the shadows, his boots resting on the coffee table. She went through the dining area. She could barely see him in the dark. His eyes were half open, his head resting back in the cushion of the chair. His hair hung a little below his shoulders, outlined by the dark short-sleeved shirt. The light of the TV lit the shiny surfaces of his shirt buttons, his belt buckle, a boot buckle, the beer can on the coffee table. She took another step, and he lifted a wad of paper over his head, moved his arm as if to shoot it—and held it.

"Foul shot," Zerk said, acknowledging her with a salute. "What do you think, Deanie?" His eyes sparkled under his drooping eyelids, and he stared as if he was waiting for her to respond. "Foul," he said. He flexed his wrist. "Foul!" he shouted. "Foul!" He banged the wall above his head. "Foul! Foul! Foul!"

"You're right," she said. Zerk brought his hand down to the arm of the chair and stared at her, his head still resting back in the cushion. "Terence told me what you told Larry's parents."

Zerk nodded. "Somebody had to. I mean, he did what he was supposed to—right? Saw a lady in distress, rode off amid cheers and applause to stop the ole dragon, and—ffffft!" He snapped his fingers. "Burned up."

As Zerk stared at her, she realized that in talking about Larry he had in a way been talking about himself. "That must have been a lot like what you went through in Vietnam."

Zerk sighed deeply and tapped the arm of the chair. "But he got burned a hundred percent, and I figure I got burned only"— he paused—"eight, nine percent." He sighed. "Them's psychic burns—they're kinda hard to measure."

"You don't have to measure them," she said, extending her arms to him. "Come here."

He nodded and began tapping his hands on the arms of the chair. "Do you want to dance?"

Deanie nodded. She could almost hear her pulse. She could barely answer him. "Yes," she whispered. "Real slow."

FOURTEEN

Deanie had been keeping to herself the last few days, taping some of the old records she'd borrowed from her parents so she'd have some tapes that she could take to Naples. After a while she seemed to fall into the music, and every so often she thought she could hear some other music below the music she happened to be taping, and before long she found herself taping all of the records in pursuit of the other music.

She had taken the records home on Sunday and come back on Monday, and the visit with her parents had been okay—but today, Tuesday, had been strange. She had taken an early train into the city for her last modeling session for August, and then, after a short wait for the elevator in the lobby of her building, the doors slid open to reveal Randall Burkhart, all by himself, smiling and picking his teeth, on his way up from a lower level, headed for his office. Seeing her, he had stuck the toothpick into his shirt pocket, and said, with a big wink, "Going my way?" and with that, something deep inside of her snapped.

"No," she had said, "not today. I won't be in today. I'm all through." And then contorting her face in disgust and lifting her hands as if she were shielding herself from something gross falling from a garbage truck, she had backed away, turned for the door, and headed for Penn Station. While she waited for the next train back to Long Island she had reflected that Randall's fate would be to spend the rest his days looking at life through one-way glass, trying to manipulate people by pressuring them to manipulate themselves. She had spent what was left of the afternoon on the beach, hoping in a vague sort of way that the sun and breeze would in some way hasten the healing of the brokenness she had begun to feel in so much of what was going on around her. Now it was early evening and she was on her way to see Susan. A little conversation and a cup of tea would, after all, she thought, be more healing than the breeze and the late August sun.

As she stepped into the kitchen she heard the shower running in the small bathroom off the utility room. She could see Barett asleep on the couch in the living room. Deanie pushed the door open and stuck her head in. "Susan, it's me, Deanie," she said, pausing, "I didn't go to work today."

"Hi," Susan said, waving her hand over the shower curtain.

"Can I make some tea?" Deanie said.

"Sure," Susan said, opening the shower curtain, "and don't wake Barett—he's sleeping in the living room."

Deanie nodded and backed away, pulling the door closed.

*   *   *

"Thanks for making the tea," Susan said, coming into the kitchen from the shower. She was flicking her fingers through her wet hair and wearing a blue terry cloth bathrobe. "Did I hear you say that you didn't go into work today?"

Deanie nodded and watched Susan move a bag of onions from the edge of the old pine trestle table and sit down across from her. Something about the onions, the handful of red and green peppers, some grapes scattered by the bowl of fruit, the black iron frying pans hanging overhead, and the lingering smells of bacon and toast made the kitchen feel really comfortable. She wanted to collect herself before she told Susan that she'd quit. "How long has Barett been sleeping?" she asked.

"Half an hour," Susan said, resting her arms on the table, "or half his life, depending on how you look at it. I'll let him sleep a while—it's so peaceful when he's sleeping."

"That's for sure," Deanie said.

"Gary's at the neighbors' house," Susan said, "their grandson is staying with them, so he has a playmate." She paused. "They really have a good time together, which is more than I can say for me and Barett."

Deanie raised her eyebrows quizzically, rested her head in her hand, and rolled a couple of grapes back and forth on the table under her fingertips. She wanted to tell Susan her news, but more than that she wanted Susan to continue about how she felt about Barett, and as she looked up Susan lifted her clasped hands to her chin and looked past her towards the door.

"Right now—at this moment—I can't separate myself any more from Barett," Susan said. "I can hardly concentrate on anything." She glanced at Deanie and folded her arms on the table. "But I did call a lawyer— a fellow I've known for some time." She breathed deeply and stared at the table. "And I've started doing what I have to do to end this mess."

Deanie didn't know what to say at first. She wasn't really surprised, but she was saddened by the fact that some marriages don't work out. "You're doing what you have to do," Deanie said, still rolling the grapes under her fingers. "But what about Gary? If you're not his mother, what then?"

"The lawyer said that, all things considered, we should be able to get Barett to agree to anything. He'll put up a good show, but in the end I think he'll be glad to let me have Gary

215

most—if not all—of the time." Susan got out her lighter and a cigarillo. "And, after all, his present responsibilities are *so much*," she added sarcastically. She put down the cigarillos and put the lighter on top of the package. "So, tell me," Susan said, "what's this about not going to your modeling session today— aren't you feeling well?"

"Well," Deanie said, "I feel okay now. I just quit a couple of weeks early. And I don't even remember much about the whole thing. I stared out the window for most of the ride in, and I remember stopping by the newsstand on my way to the office building, and then I was on the train coming back."

Susan nodded, sipped her tea, and shook out her hair. "What did Randall say?" she said.

"Nothing," Deanie said.

"What a jerk," Susan said. "He didn't say anything when he hired you, and he didn't say anything when you quit."

"I didn't give him a chance to say anything," she said. "It all went pretty fast."

"At least you made it out in one piece," Susan said.

Deanie smiled, tossed her head, and rolled the grapes under the edge of the fruit bowl, where she left them. "I guess so," she said, adjusting the collar on her shirt. "I hope so." She paused a moment and reached over to touch Susan's arm. "Are *you* going to get out in one piece?"

Susan leaned forward and slid her hands out on the table as if she were admiring them. "I'm a little worse for the wear," she said, looking at her, "but, you know, Deanie, I've got really nice hands." Susan looked back at her hands. "They used to play the cello—they could do that again. They used to type children's stories—they could do that again. They've been throwing a ball to Gary and catching it—they could certainly do more of that." She paused. "Now one of them is a cigarillo holder and the other one brushes imaginary specks from my clothes when I approach someone." She lifted her hands from the table and held them before her face. "There are going to be some changes," she said.

216

Deanie was deeply moved. "Wow," she said, "you sound like"— she paused— "a different person."

Susan smiled and sighed. "Well," she said, "after I talked to the lawyer and actually made a decision to move forward I sort of felt like a different person."

Deanie nodded. "That's really something," she said. She finished her tea, sat back, and folded her hands in her lap. "What did you do first, after you made your decision?"

Susan laughed out loud. "I went to the mall," she said, "and I bought a new pair of jeans."

"All *right*," Deanie said, laughing. "Now let me tell you about dancing with Zerk."

"*That's* more like it," Susan said.

* * *

Walking back to her place, Deanie was reflecting on her visit with Susan, how she and Barett would be separating and going in different directions. Or at least Susan would be going in a different direction. She could still see Barett asleep on the couch, still hear the gurgling sticky noises in his throat, and she realized that, unless he was able to change, his future would be to continue being the same awake as he was asleep, not recognizing the feelings of anyone around him and all the while filling the air with intrusive noises. She wondered about Gary, and then she figured that Susan's views would prevail. She knew that Gary would be better off with Susan. And then she was thinking about something else Susan had brought up. Susan had been going on about her job, and then out of nowhere she had asked her if she'd like to work for her in her office in the city two days a week—if she decided not to go to Naples. The timing of the offer had been more of a surprise than the offer itself—until Susan explained that when she had run into Zerk the other day he had mentioned that she didn't seem as enthusiastic about going to Naples as she had earlier in the summer. Deanie had answered Susan by saying that she had a lot of things on her mind, that she still planned to go to Naples. After a moment Susan asked her if she had talked with her parents about her trip. "A little," she had said, "not much. They're always very agreeable—so there's never much to really discuss about anything." Now she recalled her visit to Teaneck, seeing her father carrying her travel bag out to Susan's car, his eye pink from an accidental squirt of slide oil he'd gotten while lubricating his trombone. As he kissed her on the cheek and told her to be cool, her mother came across the driveway in her housecoat and handed her a twenty-dollar bill and a pamphlet. "Take a friend out for a pizza," she had said, "and read this." It was a pamphlet from her support group titled "Your Surgery and Ours."

*   *   *

It was eleven o'clock and Deanie was knocking on Zerk's door. She had thought about calling Kojo, but because she still hadn't heard from him she got the vague feeling that a call now would be an intrusion, so she put it off.

Just seeing Zerk's light go on raised her spirits. Now, waiting for him to come to the door, she realized that her need to talk to him, to be with him, had been growing stronger by the minute.

"Hi," Zerk said, as he pulled the door open. "Come on in."

Deanie stepped around the screen door and pushed the heavy plank door shut behind her.

"Would you like to go to Palermo with me?" she said.

She could hear him breathing. "Would I like to go to Palermo?"

"Yes"—she paused—"with me."

"Are you serious?" he said.

"Give me a break." She watched him frown and rub his forehead. "Well?" she said.

"I thought you were going to Naples."

"I am—but that's not for a couple of weeks. I'm asking you to go to Palermo *now*—Palermo, Oklahoma. Don't you remember talking about Palermo? On our walk and with that pretty sunset? The red petunias?"

"Oh." He paused. "Sure. Of course I do. But don't you have a lot of things to do for your trip to Naples?"

"I just have an informational meeting with the other people going, nothing I *have* to go to. Classes start next week, so everybody at school will be busy, but not me."

"When are you going to Palermo?" Zerk said.

"What did you say?" She hooked her thumbs over her belt and looked into his eyes.

"I said when are we going to Palermo?"

"Can you meet me Saturday at Newark Airport?"

"I have to work for a while Saturday morning. I just can't get out of it this Saturday," he said. "Really."

"You could get to the airport by the middle of the afternoon, couldn't you?"

"No sweat. There'll be holiday traffic, but I'll make it. Where are you going to be?"

"How about a ticket counter?"

"Where did you make reservations?"

"I still have to do that."

"Oh." He paused. "Why don't I just go to the United counter in Terminal A?"

"Okay. Then if I get held up I can call and leave a message there," she said.

"Okay. And if I'm early I'll hang out outside for a while. But where are you going to be coming from?"

"Newark. I'm going to try to visit Kojo and his cousins."

"How are you getting there?"

"Not to worry," she said, smiling and pushing her hair back from her face, "probably train, bus, and taxi, no problem. I knew I could count on you." She reached out and took his hands in hers. "Studying in Italy for a year, a school year, is really what I need. Maybe you can come and visit me."

219

"Maybe," he said. "I'd like to."

"And even if you can't, everything we've done will still be here," she said, letting go of his hands and crossing hers on her chest, "inside of me."

"I understand," he said.

"But sometimes I think maybe you really don't understand," she said. She felt surprise and a little sadness by what she'd said, but he was looking into her eyes, waiting for her to continue. "Sometimes you ask me how I am and I say I'm okay, but you should know when I don't mean it."

"That's not easy," he said.

"Well," she said, "maybe it isn't. But..." She shrugged.

"But what?" he said.

She leaned over and put her arms around him. *I'm so tired, so very tired.* "I don't have the energy," she said.

"I love you," he said, holding her, and pulling her closer.

She closed her eyes. Those three words were right there inside her. She could almost see them, but they wouldn't come out. She wouldn't let them come out. Not right now. Not now. Not now. And with a start the notion crossed her mind that maybe they couldn't come out. "Oh, Zerk," she said, "I have to be going. I'll let you know about the tickets."

* * *

After Deanie got back to her place she sat there in her living room, lit only by dim light from the kitchen, wondering if she would call to make her reservations or wait. She lay back on the sofa and shut her eyes. She would have to stop by the bank in the next couple of days and cash a check. Maybe Shelley could drive her to the train station Saturday morning. It would be nice if somebody with a limo would pick her up...and then pick up Zerk...and Kojo...her eyes opened drowsily and closed.

* * *

220

It was around seven o'clock Wednesday evening as Shelley dropped Deanie off at the Sanborn estate. They had spent the afternoon on the beach on the south shore near Amagansett. Earlier in the day when she had told Shelley that she was going to fly off to Palermo, Oklahoma, with Zerk, she had responded to Shelley's quizzical look by showing her a picture she'd torn from an old copy of the *National Geographic Magazine* that she had found in a box of magazines in the gatehouse. "Oh, I see," Shelley had said, looking at the sunny park, the vague shapes of a city in the distance, "*that's* Palermo, Oklahoma. But where in the hell *is* it?" Deanie had shaken her head and said, "It's out there. And I can get there." And then Shelley had rolled her eyes and said she'd give her a ride to the train station if she really wanted one.

Now Deanie was going to check her mailbox before going back to the gatehouse. The mailbox was filled with back-to-school advertising and flyers for Labor Day sales. She pulled everything out and carried it all around the gatepost towards the porch. As she walked across the grass she kicked off her sandals and pulled the blue and white beach towel off her shoulders and tossed it over the sawhorse on the porch. She set her bag on the bricks, and, sitting on the bottom step, began looking through the bundle of mail.

There was a notice about the final "Junior Year in Italy" meeting, something from the financial aid office, something from the library, and a valentine postcard. That's funny, she thought, wondering why the card was there. It had her name and address written with a pen. She looked at the message.

> Deanie,
> I hope you're well.
> See you soon.
> K—

"'K'?" she said aloud. "Who's 'K'?" She looked at the red, white, and green cartoon on the other side. There was a smiling

221

heart-person running up a mountain, and in his reaching red-gloved hand was a heart-stamped envelope that said "A Love Letter for You." "Kojo," she whispered. "You remembered." She took a deep breath—it felt like pure oxygen. Now she could call him and let him know that she was coming. She took another breath. She didn't know what he meant by "soon," but she knew what she meant.

Going up the stairs to her apartment, Deanie dug in her pocket for Kojo's phone number. She hoped she could get hold of him. She hoped she could see him Saturday on her way to Palermo, Oklahoma.

FIFTEEN

As the cab moved slowly past the narrowly-spaced tan, gray, and dark-green frame houses shaded by maples, Deanie watched the house numbers going down to the one Kojo had given her over the phone. A boy as dark as Kojo, about nine or ten, in shorts and barefoot, sat on the porch steps, tapping drumsticks on a large clay flowerpot.

The house was slate-gray with dark-red trim. A piece of unfinished plywood covered the lower half of the first-floor window by the porch, and to the right of it was a red and white "Beware of the Dog" sign. On the first step, above the flowerpot, was an orange and black plastic jack-o'-lantern the size of a basketball.

The cabdriver wiped a towel across his glistening neck, mopping the rivulets of sweat that trickled from his pork-chop sideburns. He put the towel back on the seat, and Deanie dropped the fare and tip into the palm of his hand and opened the door. She adjusted the shoulder strap of her little leather bag, straightened her sleeveless blouse, pulled the canvas travel bag off the seat, and turned to see Kojo coming down the driveway, followed by the boy with the drumsticks.

Kojo was wearing shades, a red and black dashiki, tan cotton pants, and sneakers. He stepped around a bicycle lying on the patch of grass between the driveway and the sidewalk and extended his hand to take her travel bag. "You made it," he said, lifting his eyebrows and nodding, "in good time."

She nodded and hooked her thumbs over the top of her jeans. "The bus from New York to Newark was a little slow because of the Labor Day weekend, but for the most part it was a good trip."

"Are you and Zerk still off to Oklahoma this afternoon?"

"Palermo, Oklahoma," she said.

"Is that near Oklahoma City?"

"It's not on the map."

Kojo glanced away a moment and looked back, frowning, his index finger pointed up and pressed against the front of his goatee. "It's not on the map?" He tapped his finger against his goatee. "I see," he said. "It's *that* kind of a trip?"

She nodded. "Yes," she said. "It is. But I'll be back in plenty of time to go to Naples."

"I understand," he said, smiling. "Not to worry. Come. You must meet my cousins." He started up the concrete driveway that was squeezed between his cousins' house and the neighbors' small frame house on the other side. The September sky was a little hazy and between the peaks of the two houses she saw a silver speck, a single plane way in the distance.

The boy walked past them and picked up the bicycle.

"Thanks again for the love letter," Deanie said.

Kojo laughed a low mellow laugh. "I'm glad it cheered you up a bit," he said.

"I'm glad you didn't get any serious injuries," she said.

"So am I." He made a rolling gesture with his hand. "By Sunday afternoon, I was pretty sure I had nothing more than a cracked rib—though I still wanted to rest my back a bit. At any rate, I called a friend in the city and he picked me up on Monday morning."

"Why didn't you call me for a ride?"

"Well"—he paused—"I didn't want to bother anyone around Peeze after everything that had happened, and I'd promised my cousins that I'd be here Monday." He gestured with his hand as if to indicate that's all there was to say and adjusted his shades.

"But how could you bother me?" she said.

"I thought you'd been through enough for a while."

"That's disappointing."

"I certainly didn't mean to make you feel bad," he said. "I'm sorry if I did."

"Friends are supposed to help friends."

"I'm sorry you felt bad."

"That's okay," she said. "I just thought you might've thought I couldn't take it. I feel better now—especially being away from Peeze."

"I can certainly empathize with you on that," he said. "Kindred spirits." He smiled and nodded a couple of times.

"That's what I thought. And if we're kindred spirits, will you tell me something?"

"What?"

"What did Susan mean when she said you could go buy the guns yourself?"

"Didn't you hear me say that she was having fantasies?"

"Yes."

"Well." He paused. "Ask me no questions and I'll tell you no lies."

"You sound just like Carl Peterson," she said, shaking her head. "That's his standard answer when he's in a predicament."

Kojo laughed and adjusted his sunglasses. "To follow in the line you've suggested," he said, adjusting his sunglasses again, "let me say that I'm not in a predicament, and I don't want either of us to get into one."

The boy rode past her, cut over to the grass behind the house, circled around the sandbox, and stopped next to the brown van parked in front of the single-car garage. He frowned and scratched his bare chest.

225

"What's his name?"

"That's David, my cousin's son."

"Hello, David," she said. He stopped frowning, took hold of the handlebar grips, and turned one as if he were revving a motorcycle.

Kojo touched her arm and stopped by the corner of the house as two young men came out, one in a green and gold dashiki, jeans, and brown loafers, one in a loose-fitting dark-blue shirt that he wore out over black pants, and sneakers. "This is my friend Deanie," he said, "and, Deanie, this is Victor, David's father"—the fellow in the dashiki nodded—"and Amega." Amega nodded and looked at Kojo. "Deanie is going to ride to the airport with us." The two men frowned and stared at Kojo. "We're giving her a ride to Terminal A where she's catching a flight with a friend of hers."

Having heard that, the cousins seemed to relax, and Amega opened the door, startling a little girl who had been watching them. She was about five or six and had at least a dozen yellow bows on little braids all over her head. Deanie watched her run from the back porch to a young woman standing in the kitchen. Seeing crayons, scissors, and cut-up greeting cards on the porch floor, Deanie imagined that Kojo had gotten the valentine from her.

"That's Amega's daughter, Adisa," Kojo said, "and her mother, Betty." He swung Deanie's travel bag towards the door. "Let's go inside and have a cool drink and something to eat before we go to the airport. Betty has baked some fine bean cake for us."

Inside, Deanie smelled coffee brewing and chicken frying, and as she stepped into the kitchen the little girl pulled her mother's pink plaid dress across the lower half of her face like a veil and stared at her.

*   *   *

"I'm glad your van has air conditioning," Deanie said.

"Amega installed it himself," Kojo said.

Amega glanced back from the wheel and nodded. Victor was next to him, and Deanie and Kojo sat on a cushioned bench that was built lengthwise along the right side of the van. They were moving along the expressway, heading for Newark Airport where, as Kojo had said at lunch, they were going to deliver to a freight terminal some tools to be shipped to Ghana.

Deanie rested back in the cushion, her hands in her front pockets, her legs straight out, her feet resting on the canvas that covered the crates of tools stacked in the center of the van. The only windows were in the two front doors and the two doors in back, and as she talked with Kojo, sitting on her right, she from time to time glanced out Amega's window at the sides of passing trucks—"Mayflower...Pittsburgh...Eskimo Pie"—and now and then seeing part of a sign, a section of smokestack, she tried to guess how close they were to the airport.

"Tell me," Kojo asked, "how did you happen to choose Palermo, Oklahoma?"

"I didn't really *choose* it," she said. "It's something that came up a while back when I was talking with Zerk, and I guess my desire to go there has been growing all summer. I finally felt I had to go, and since you were here I thought I could see you and fly out of Newark."

"You must be very close to Zerk to invite him along on such a fantastic journey," Kojo said, smiling.

"We're friends," she said, glancing out the window, "close friends," and turning to Kojo she smiled as he gave her a thumbs-up sign.

"That is good," he said.

She nodded and looked out the window, suddenly remembering that Susan had asked her for Kojo's Newark phone number—which she had avoided giving her.

"I meant to tell you," she said, "that when Susan found out that I was going to visit you she asked for your phone number—but I got out of giving it to her by saying that you had called me."

227

"Damn," he said. Kojo rested his head back in the cushion and folded his hands in his lap. He seemed to be thinking over what she had just told him.

"Do you know why she wanted it?" she asked.

"No—though I think she's trying to hold onto something," he said.

"Something like the afterimage of the notebook?" Deanie said. He nodded. "And she hasn't blinked enough for it to go away?"

He nodded again. "That's a good way to put it," he said.

"And there's something else," she said.

"Something else?"

"Susan told me that she's contacted a lawyer to start getting a divorce," she said.

"Is that so?"

Deanie nodded. "She told me Tuesday."

"Well," Kojo said, "I hope things work out for her." He looked towards Amega and Victor and rested back in the cushion.

Deanie nodded. "So do I," she said. She rested her head back and looked at the crates stacked in front of her. They were starting to make her nervous. The way they looked, covered with the canvas, made the whole thing look a little like a casket, and she moved her feet to the carpeted floor. "What kind of tools do you have here?"

Amega turned around. "A variety of tools," he said, "for many things." He turned back to the wheel. "To help get things built—schools, houses, power plants."

Kojo rolled his head towards the other two. Deanie noticed him tapping his foot on the carpet as if he was becoming impatient with something. She rested her head back. She wondered how Zerk was doing—she checked her watch, it was a little after one. "Are you dropping me or the tools off first?" she asked.

"You," Victor snapped.

His response made her feel a little uneasy.

"We'll see," Kojo said.

Victor and Amega looked at each other a moment and turned back to the windshield. Kojo seems to have the last word here, she thought. That's a relief.

"Where did you get the tools?" she said. Kojo tipped his head back as if he was pondering an answer. She wondered if her questions were making them uptight. She hoped not. She wondered if they had a place like Palermo, Oklahoma, where they could go when they wanted to. She watched orange, white, and yellow smoke billowing from factory stacks receding in the distance. They must be coming up on the airport. It couldn't be too far away...

"As far as getting the tools," Kojo said, "we had a connection with a wholesaler on a wharf in Bayonne." He paused as he pulled his feet back to the edge of the bench and folded his arms over his chest. "And now we're sending them home."

"Won't that be awfully expensive?" she said. "Air freight for that distance can't be cheap."

Amega said something to Victor in tone language.

"It would be expensive," Kojo said, "but they're going to be moved to another storage place, and then later on they'll be shipped to Ghana on a freighter."

"A freighter to Ghana," she said. "That sounds exciting."

"I'd prefer to fly," Kojo said. "Freighters aren't very exciting."

"I bet they could be," she said.

Victor said something to Amega in tone language and he nodded.

"Of course, freighters could be exciting," Kojo said to her. "And you could even charter one to Palermo, Oklahoma."

"That's right," she said, resting her head back in the cushion. But maybe she'd charter a ship to someplace else, some other time. Now she was flying to Palermo, Oklahoma, with Zerk. She was glad that she was giving some shape to her life that went beyond getting from one point to another on a map. She

229

could live with uncertainties, but that didn't always work unless she could shape their context, which included herself, or part of herself—and that must be where the paintings and sculptures come in, she told herself, appearing on windows and walls when she was anxious and trying to give shape to things. Cows and eyes and breasts and the horse made of the beach blanket and elbows and hair... Now and then, she reflected, it was as if something inside her made her see as she imagined a cubist might see to get from one end of the day to the other. Once again she saw the female form growing through the taxi windshield, all kinds of things. She saw the horse made of her beach blanket and towels and the mirrored shades—galloping down a distant valley and up a faraway hill into shadow. And looking back in the direction from which they all came, it seemed that they all had come somehow from some impossible thing—like a four-sided triangle, or an eight-sided cube—the kind of thing Randall Burkhart was forever looking for, but would never find unless somehow it thought in him or he thought in it.

Victor said something in tone language and Amega laughed and Kojo shook his head.

Kojo turned to Deanie. "He was wondering if you were thinking of something exciting."

"Why?" she said.

"Pay no attention to Victor," Amega said, "we don't need any excitement."

Kojo took off his shades and tapped them on the seat cushion. Nodding at her he smiled and pointed the shades at Victor. "He has a woman in New York who cannot be kept waiting," he said, with a deep gentle laugh.

"But why are you saying we don't need any excitement?" she asked.

Amega tensed up, his forearm muscles rippling as he gripped the steering wheel. He seemed to be ignoring her. He said something in tone language very loud and looked from Victor to

Kojo and back to his side-view mirror, and Victor took out a cigarette and lit it.

Deanie sat up and gestured towards Kojo. "What's the matter?" she said.

"Amega's concerned about a state trooper behind us."

"Is that a problem?" she said.

Kojo shook his head. "Not to worry."

Looking at the canvas-covered crates, Deanie began to think that the tools were probably not the kind that Kojo would want inspected under the circumstances, and she knew that the highway patrol had been stopping vans and hippie-looking vehicles all summer. She pressed her fingertips to her temples. Shit, she said to herself, three black guys and me and a load of guns. If a cop stops us he'll call for help and they'll go through everything.

"Why don't you let me drive?" she said.

"What?" Kojo said.

"If he stops us for any reason and sees me in here with the three of you, he'll take a good look around, and"—she leaned closer to Kojo—"if you're keeper of the tools, you can't let him do that."

Kojo's eyes narrowed. "Keeper of the tools," he said, his face softening to a gentle smile. "Deanie, you're too much."

Kojo said something in tone language and Victor put his foot on the accelerator pedal and held the wheel as Amega and Deanie traded places. She could reach the pedals—she didn't have to adjust the seat. It felt just like the van her father used to bring home from the store. The side-view mirrors were okay. She saw Kojo and Amega in the rear-view mirror and flipped her hair over her shoulders. Nobody said anything as Deanie drove towards the airport.

Now the trooper was pulling into the left lane, coming up beside her, and before she knew it she was counting the clicks and thumps her tires made on the bumps in the road, and looking down at the police car she saw the trooper's right leg, the coiled mike wire running up along his raised elbow past his shoulder.

231

She couldn't see any higher; she couldn't tell whether or not he was looking at the van. She looked at Victor. His head was back in the seat, his arms lay across his lap, a strand of cigarette smoke rising from his hand. She checked the speedometer; she had been slowing down; she picked it up and held it at 50; the trooper was still right there, still on his radio, and she was doing all right. She looked in her side-view mirror and saw something coming up behind the police car, pulling out and coming ahead. She glanced back at Kojo; he had his shades back on and appeared to be watching her. Amega sat leaning way over to his left looking out the back windows and where his shirt had pulled up she saw the pistol stuck inside his pants. Suddenly the thing behind the police car was a horse pulling out and passing it. It was a huge stuffed animal made of her old jeans, her father's tan work shirts, her mother's bandages, record album covers, all wired together with coils from her spiral-bound notebooks. It kept getting bigger and bigger. There were patches of striped wallpaper from her room at home, pressed flowers, old report cards, a pillowcase from a motel, letters from her grandmother, paycheck stubs from Burkhart Modeltronics, an Italian grammar book, and sitting sidesaddle, facing the sky, was a big cut-out photograph of herself, and she was rocking in the van seat, and the horse was going faster and faster and flying up high into the sun, and suddenly the police car shot ahead, roaring in passing gear, a jet of black exhaust bursting from the tailpipe—and he was gone. "All right," she said, throwing her hand out to Victor. "He kept on going."

Victor took her hand. "Nice work," he said.

"That's what we have to do," Kojo said.

Deanie glanced back. "What?"

"Keep on going."

Hearing that, she expected him to lift his eyebrows and nod vigorously, but he just sat there looking very calm behind his shades, and Amega nodded a couple of times.

The road into the airport curved away from the highway and after a hundred yards began branching through patches of grass and weeds browned by exhaust. All along the way signs rose up and leaned, pointing to terminals and offices and lots that seemed to stretch past the airport all the way east to Port Newark and Port Elizabeth.

"Bear to your right," Kojo said.

A plane roared overhead and she instinctively ducked as she turned to check Victor's side-view mirror. Down in front of her she noticed the air-freshener card hanging on a string from the radio knob. It was in the shape of a tulip, red and green, and lilac-scented. She checked her side-view mirror as she began moving with the trucks and vans headed for the freight docks among the metal-sided hangars and warehouses up ahead. A gray truck passed her and she slowed down to let it move into her lane. She glanced at her three passengers. They all seemed composed, alert. Kojo seemed to be looking out Victor's side of the windshield, at a point somewhere above the horizon. Out of the corner of her eye she saw the air-freshener again. Shaped like a tulip, she said to herself, and scented like lilacs. She wondered why it wasn't tulip-scented, or shaped like a cluster of lilacs. Ahead the road spread like spilled tar into the weeds and around the trucks and past the metal buildings. She glanced up at the rear-view mirror. Kojo had his hands clasped behind his neck, his elbows raised, his head resting back in the cushion. And as she looked back at the road it struck her that from that angle his upper outline had looked for an instant like the upper outline of the tulip. Looks like one kind of flower, smells like another kind of flower. What kind of flower is it? Looking back at the mirror she wondered how far the comparison would go—but he had moved. She glanced back. Kojo was sitting up and looking over Victor's shoulder.

"Pull over," Victor said, pointing towards the roadside, "right here."

Deanie checked the mirrors and pulled off the road and sat with her foot on the brake. "Why do you want me to stop?" she asked, turning past Victor to Kojo.

233

"I get out here," Kojo said. Victor leaned out of his way and opened the door. Kojo stepped around him and put his hand on her shoulder. "Thank you, Deanie," he said. "I have a class Tuesday, so I'll see you when you get back. Not to worry." He gripped her shoulder a little tighter and leaning away he let go and jumped out. She reached up to her shoulder where his hand had been. She was surprised, but not alarmed. She started to say "Take care," but for some reason she couldn't get it out and then he was out of sight.

Victor pulled the door closed and shifted around towards her. "Let's go," he said, pointing towards a tan warehouse a hundred yards down the road.

"Okay," she said. She saw Amega watching her, checked her side mirror, and saw Kojo striding up the road. She leaned out and turned back to see him straight on, his head high, the red and black dashiki rippling in the wind. She wanted to ask where he was going, but when she thought about it she figured it would be better to wait. She turned back, pulled onto the road and took off. And for that matter, she thought, maybe Kojo was going someplace like Palermo, Oklahoma, and there wouldn't be any point in asking Victor and Amega about something like that, something so personal. As she approached the entrance to the warehouse lot she checked her mirrors. Kojo wasn't in sight. She couldn't wait any longer. "Where's he going?" she asked.

"Back to work," Victor said. Deanie glanced at him and nodded. She wouldn't ask again.

"He has a calling," Amega said.

She looked in the rear-view mirror to see Amega. "He certainly does," she said. He recognized her with a salute and she nodded and looked back to the road. "He certainly does," she whispered to herself.

"Slow down," Victor said. She let up on the gas and braked for the turn. "That way," he said, pointing. "Over there. Pull around and back up to the overhead door."

Deanie pulled past the corner of the building, stopped, and leaned out her window to see where she was backing the van.

She stopped about twenty feet from the overhead door and looked at Victor. "Just back in?" she said.

He nodded. "When the door opens back right inside."

"Okay," she said. She saw Victor holding a remote door-opener, the door going up, and she backed into the warehouse. There were a lot of boxes stacked on pallets and parked off to the side was a bright yellow forklift truck that looked brand new. Zerk would love to have that, she said to herself. Come to think of it, he should be in the terminal by now, waiting for me.

"You can shut it off," Victor said, opening his door, "and get out and stretch."

Deanie switched off the ignition and watched Amega pull the canvas off the crates and step back to unlatch the rear doors and throw them open. She picked up her bags, decided to leave them on the seat, and as she slid off the seat the closing overhead door reached the floor. She jumped down and walked towards the rear of the van.

"Stop!" someone shouted.

She froze. It sounded like Victor. She couldn't see anyone past the open rear door and from nowhere someone in black coveralls and a ski mask spun past her in the ear-splitting bangs of gunshots to spin again shooting to hit Victor, who fell past her to hit the floor. The person wearing the mask spun again to face her and a bang exploded blood from his coveralls rolling him over to flop against a box in a red slide to the floor. His gun lay by his feet. It was a shotgun and she saw another movement on her left, someone aiming a pistol towards her. She saw Amega leaning from the van, his pistol out, both pistols firing. Now she had the shotgun up *and pointing at the coffee can head pulled the front trigger and now the rear one and fired seeing the coffee can head burst open,* and she turned back to Amega and saw his arm hanging down across the bumper, blood dripping from his finger into a growing puddle of gas from the van.

She stood back against the truck, wondering if anybody else was there. Were the others alive or dead? Or what? She couldn't hear anything. Her ears were ringing. She couldn't hear a thing. She checked Amega's wrist. No pulse. She looked around, didn't see anybody. She couldn't hear a thing. She walked over to Victor. He'd got it from the first attacker. Now what? Her ears were ringing like crazy. Destroy the ringing. Destroy the evidence, she told herself. She put down the shotgun and not looking at Victor's bloody head took the lighter from his shirt pocket. She looked at the shotgun. Fingerprints. But her fingerprints were all over the truck. She had to do something. What had Kojo said? Cut across the grain if you have to, but don't cut yourself? Something like that. She pulled Victor's handkerchief from his pocket, wiped the shotgun, and walked over to the second attacker. Sliding the sleeve up from the glove she saw how small the wrist was and feeling no pulse looked at the wrist again and gasping in surprise she leaned closer to the remains of the ski mask and lifting the edge saw the cheek, the ear, the long blond hair, and now the body was clearly female, somebody around her own age, and she stood up, and backing away turned for the van. Now she had to check the first attacker and seeing the wound in the chest she knew there was no pulse and seeing the beard on the neck she knew this one wasn't a woman. She turned and ran to the open driver's door and stopped. "What do I want?" she said. She saw her bags. She pulled her bags out and slid the straps over her shoulder. "Now what?" She saw Victor's handkerchief in her hand and dropped it. She ran to the front door of the warehouse, opened the bolt, pushed it open, and turned and ran back inside. "Paper, paper, paper, paper," she said looking for something to torch the gas under the van.

*   *   *

Deanie cleared the doorway and slammed the door an instant before the whole thing blew up. The size of the warehouse contained the explosion and now she was running towards the terminal, and looking back she could see smoke rising from a vent just below the roof line. She stopped to wipe the sweaty hair from her face before going on towards the terminal, and moving out of the way for a truck she turned to see the side door of the warehouse fly across the lot and heard another explosion now blowing flames through the doorway. She shook her head, her ears still ringing, hitched up the shoulder straps, turned for the terminal, and ran.

She had been running a long time when she saw Zerk up ahead on the sidewalk coming at her with his arms out, his bag at his side. She ran to him. Now she was resting her head on his shoulder, gasping for breath, looking up at his startled face.

"Where have you been?" he asked. She could feel the alarm in his voice, but she couldn't answer. After a moment she pointed towards the warehouse and saw the smoke.

"Palermo, Oklahoma," she said. She had wanted to say something else, but that's all that came out.

"That's why I'm here," he said. He took her travel bag, shouldered the strap, and reached for her hand. "Are you okay?" She nodded and turned towards the terminal and they started walking.

"I can't believe what happened," she said. "Kojo and his cousins gave me a ride..." She realized that she was shaking all over. "And you wouldn't believe what happened."

"Is Kojo okay?"

"He said not to worry."

"You can tell me about it later," Zerk said. He hitched up the bags' shoulder straps and put his arm around her waist. "Do you think we're going to find a flight to Palermo, Oklahoma?"

"Of course." She paused a moment. "Though some other name might be printed on the tickets."

"Of course," he said.

She rested her head on his shoulder. "You're still with me?"

"Always."

ABOUT THE AUTHOR

Tom Gatten's fiction has appeared in such publications as *Art and Literature* (Lausanne), *The Quest* (New York), and *Tales*, formerly *Fiction Midwest* (St. Louis). His poems have appeared in numerous publications and have been anthologized in *The Sumac Reader* (The Michigan State University Press, East Lansing), and *Earth, Air, Fire & Water* (Coward, McCann & Geohegan, New York, and Longmans Canada Limited, Toronto). His book of poems and translations, *Mapper of Mists*, includes the Spanish of Rafael Alberti.

Tom Gatten was born in north central Nebraska and grew up in southwestern Michigan. While a grad student at Michigan State University he played for two years with the Bamboushay Steel Band (Folkways Records LP FS 3835). After Michigan State he went to the University of Iowa, where he earned an M.F.A. His college teaching credits include Fresno, Stony Brook, Lincoln Land Community College, The University of Hartford, and Penn State. He lives in central Pennsylvania with his wife.

Printed in the United States
2301